To Dr. Rodgers from
Thanks for your help and special
medical work.
Bill

Are You a Real Doctor?

Also by Mark DePaolis

"Trust Me, I'm a Doctor"

Get Well Sooner

Are You a Real Doctor?

*More Humorous Second Opinions
for Everyday Life*

MARK DEPAOLIS

FAIRVIEW PRESS   *Minneapolis*

ARE YOU A REAL DOCTOR? © 1997 Mark DePaolis. All rights reserved. No part of this publication may be used or reproduced in any manner whatsoever without written permission, except in the case of brief quotations embodied in critical articles and reviews. For further information, please contact the publisher.

Published by Fairview Press, 2450 Riverside Avenue South, Minneapolis, MN 55454

Library of Congress Cataloging-in-Publication Data

DePaolis, Mark, 1956–
    Are you a real doctor? : more humorous second opinions for everyday life / Mark DePaolis.
    p.   cm.
    ISBN 1–57749–028–2 (alk. paper)
    1. Medicine—Humor.   I. Title.
PN6231.M4D45   1997
814'.54—dc21   96–29732

First Printing: March 1997

Printed in the United States of America
01 00 99 98 97   7 6 5 4 3 2 1

Cover design: Circus Design

Publisher's Note: Fairview Press publishes books and other materials related to the subjects of physical health, mental health, and chemical dependency. Its publications, including *Are You a Real Doctor?*, do not necessarily reflect the philosophy of Fairview Hospital and Healthcare Services or their treatment programs.

For a free catalogue, call toll-free 1–800–544–8207.

"A Klingon Walk with Thee" appeared previously in *New York Newsday*. "Home Healing," "Closing in on Jargon," "Where No Doctor Has Gone Before," "What's in the Pockets?," "The TV News Doctor Audition," "Paging the Rug Doctor," "Dr. Mom," "My Doctor, Myself," "Who's Really in Charge," "Stranger in Surgery," "The Big Bird Doctor Kit," "When Doctors Get Sick," and "My Doctor, the Son" appeared previously in *Postgraduate Medicine*. The remaining essays appeared previously in the Minneapolis *Star Tribune*.

For Rosa, my wife,

who is much funnier than me

Contents

Foreword by Eric Ringham	x
Aerobics: Just Do It, Badly	1
Smooth "Operation"	4
Having the Sex Talk with Your Child	7
Dress Me Up, Dress Me Down	10
Real-Life Medical Revivals	13
Moles—Should You Tell?	16
Mud Slinging at the Health Spa	19
TV Doctor Shows Get Really Real	22
Women's Shoes: The Fashionable Menace	26
Coffee Is Hot	29
Old TV Stars? Book 'Em	32
High-Tech Cooling Trend	35
Women Are from Venus, Menopause from Mars	38
Power Rangers—Yes or No?	41
Home Healing	45

Closing In on Jargon	48
Fun at the Casino? Don't Bet on It	51
An Aspirin a Day Keeps the Cardiologist Away	54
Where No Doctor Has Gone Before	57
What's in the Pockets?	61
Act Like a Doctor	64
Nerd Processing—Computers in Medicine	67
Dr. Superman	70
Dental Plan	73
Fitting into Your Fat Genes	76
The TV News Doctor Audition	79
Paging the Rug Doctor	83
Medical Christmas Shopping	87
Dr. Mark's Fun-Time Clinic	91
Infection Reflection	94
Dr. Mom	97
Life Lessons on the Ant Farm	100
Back to the Basics	103
A Klingon Walk with Thee	106
Blood Tests for Vampires	110
Physicals Attraction	114
Doctors on the Bat-Line	117
Back-to-School Supplies	120
New Hope for Depression	123
Surgeon General-less	126
Head Lice Aren't Nice	129
A Guide to Confusing Medical Reports	132
New Ulcer Medicines Hard to Swallow	135
Exercising Your Options	138
My Doctor, Myself	141
Stranger in Surgery	144
Fertility, Guaranteed	147

Acknowledgments

Once again I want to thank my editor at the *Star Tribune*, Eric Ringham, who edits my column to make me look funnier than I really am. I am especially grateful that he wrote a brilliant, hilarious introduction to this book so I didn't have to.

Thanks also to Susan Albright at the *Star Tribune*, who allows my column to appear on the Editorial Page instead of getting stuck between the horoscopes and Beetle Bailey. And to editor Sue Wolkerstorfer, who laughs out loud twice each time.

I also want to thank my colleagues and co-workers at Park Nicollet Clinic, who are always answering my questions and coming with ideas for columns, which I then use as my own. And the nurses and receptionists who work in our office, who have to handle more than their share of weird phone calls on Fridays when my column appears.

And a special thanks to my friend Michelle Thayer, who bought hundreds of copies of my first book when she wasn't even mentioned. Just imagine how many she'll buy this time

Foreword

might have shared his (and my) interest in comic books. Among my other doctor acquaintances, one is an opera buff and another is seriously, even gravely, into Irish poetry. Mark never misses *Lois & Clark*.

As a guest on a radio talk show, Mark was asked whether he'd heard what killed George Burns, who had died a day or two before. "Yep," Mark replied. "He was 100."

Of all the doctors I know, he's the one who takes himself least seriously. He tends to assume that sick people will get better eventually, with or without his help. That alone would make most other doctors want to see his credentials. I've known him to pay house calls, which would make them howl for his license. Sometimes when my family goes to his house for dinner, dessert is followed by a round of exams to see if the kids have ear infections. Come for the pie—stay for the amoxicillin.

Never once has he complained when I've edited his columns, which suggests he's not a doctor, and he answers correctly every science question in Trivial Pursuit, which suggests he is. When he saw my family had only a Fisher Price stethoscope, he provided us with a real one, which suggests he is a doctor, but he didn't bill us for it, which suggests he's not.

Read the book and decide for yourself. Can real doctors do the things Mark does? Can they both take care of people and make them laugh? Can they write columns as well as prescriptions? Do they perform equally well in an examining room and in a comedy club? Do they find it possible to reconcile their oath to do no harm with an ambition to knock 'em dead?

The good ones do.

Eric Ringham
Commentary Editor
Star Tribune

Foreword

Nobody has asked more often than I whether Mark DePaolis is a real doctor. The evidence is conflicting.

He has a sense of humor, which suggests he's not a real doctor. His phone is sometimes answered by a nurse, which suggests he is a real doctor, and sometimes by himself, which suggests he's not.

"Of course I'm an M.D.," he says. Big deal. Those are his initials. I'm an E.R., but that doesn't make me an emergency room.

He writes well, which suggests he's not a real doctor, but illegibly, which suggests he is. He does stand-up comedy, which most doctors don't, but he tries out his material on people one at a time in little rooms, and all doctors do that.

Once I called him at the office and Deb, his nurse, answered the phone. "He's with a patient," she said. "I'll get him." A long time later Mark came on the line, sounding shaken. "You wouldn't believe what I was just doing," he said. I didn't inquire further because I know the kind of thing that grosses him out. There is a whole class of medical procedures that in his head are filed under O, for "ooky." Do real doctors get grossed out?

Marcus Welby would smile kindly and say, "The good ones do."

Mark is like no TV doctor, although I suppose Doogie Howser

Primary Care for Your Lawn	150
Keeping Up with Medical Breakthroughs	153
Virtual Colons	157
Waist Not	160
HMO Knows	163
A Nose for Nicotine	166
Germs by Mail	169
The Big Bird Doctor Kit	173
When Doctors Get Sick	176
Holiday Time	179
Crazy for Cholesterol	182
Sit-Down Doctor	185
Back to School	188
Quick! To the Bloodmobile!	191
Health to the Chief	194
All Alone on Career Day	197
Death Mail	200
Rating the Nielsens	203
Everyday Olympics	206
My Doctor, the Son	209

Aerobics: Just Do It, Badly

I am a firm believer in the benefits of exercise when no one can see you.

In the summer, this is easy. I can spend my afternoons running through the gentle countryside, communing with small woodland creatures, the quiet stillness of the forest broken only when I stop at the end to vomit.

Things are trickier in the winter. The ground is covered with ice, which makes running like playing some grisly video game where instead of three "lives" you get two knees. The woodland creatures have all gone to Florida, where they work as extras in Orlando theme parks until spring. Add to this the feeling when your nose hairs freeze shut, and you'll see why I spend the winter exercising indoors.

Some people do this with an exercise machine. The most popular type is the cross-country ski machine, which allows you to simulate this excellent form of exercise while watching old *Star Trek* episodes. Machines like these provide cardiovascular conditioning, muscle toning, and a place to hang clothes in the corner of the basement once you realize how boring they are.

Another option is to join a health club. There they have more expensive exercise equipment, which is professionally adjusted and maintained to have no clothes hanging on it. They also have exercise classes, which they use to encourage people to stay home and send in their monthly fee by check.

Not all these classes involve actual exercise. I know because my wife once accidentally went to a class in yoga. (Like many Americans, my only knowledge of yoga can be summed up by the phrase "Hey, hey, BooBoo, grab the pic-a-nic basket before the Ranger comes.")

It turns out that yoga is the type of exercise class where they give you—honest—a blanket. People at the class were supposedly deep in meditation, focused on physical awareness and mind-induced relaxation techniques. My wife slept for thirty minutes, then had a cool-down period. People were coming up to her afterward saying, "Wow, you're really good—are you sure this is your first time?"

Other classes, like aerobics, are much more active, giving you all the benefits of an organized, indoor, repetitive, high-intensity, low-impact workout—you know, girl exercise.

This is not based on any sexist anti-aerobicism on my part, but on the people going to these classes. There are usually about twenty women for every man, who is only there because he is on a date.

Exercising in a group like this means making a few changes, especially in attire. I usually select my exercise clothes by odor and stiffness, rejecting any items that seem to be made out of fiberglass instead of fabric. Aerobics, on the other hand, is a lycra-intensive sport, and many people wear clothing so tight it does not permit sweat to escape from their skin pores. The exercise itself is also different. During running your mind tends to wander, your thoughts drifting inward until they gradually fix on one overriding question: when will you be done? The movements are simple, consisting entirely of (1) pick up a foot, (2) put it back down, (3) repeat until delusional.

Aerobics: Just Do It, Badly

In aerobics you have to watch what everyone else is doing. Your biggest worry is being out of step. Most aerobics teachers are professional exercisers who do three high-impact classes before lunch. Now you have to imitate everything they do, including grin and be perky. This is like watching a Fred Astaire movie at home and trying to follow along.

It all adds up to quite a workout, and not just mentally. Aerobics is excellent exercise for muscles you never knew you had, like the ones inside your thighs. These never get much attention in normal life. Aerobics also includes specific exercises for areas like "the pones," which are important to keep in shape even though, according to my anatomy books, they do not exist.

But that's not the point. Aerobics is more than just exercise. It is a complex series of choreographed movements in a prearranged sequence. It is not unlike dancing, only they can't call it that or men would never come.

Besides, it's all good for you. There is no such thing as bad exercise, only exercise that makes you feel like a clumsy, uncoordinated, middle-aged dweeb with absolutely no sense of rhythm.

This is why I'm especially glad when I see warm weather making a comeback. Then I can go back to exercising outside, alone, until it's finally "game over" for my knees. At that point, my wife can prop me in the corner of the basement. Later, when she realizes how boring I am, I'm sure she will hang some clothes on me.

Smooth "Operation"

I've been feeling great these days, thanks to my Operation—the game, not the medical procedure.

I played Operation as a kid, and I was surprised to find it on the shelf while shopping for a gift. As often happens while shopping for other people, I saw it and immediately thought of myself. It just seemed so right. That's how you can tell the perfect gift—you buy two and keep one.

Most adults remember the game. It was invented in 1965, I like to think by Dr. Milton Bradley, although no one at the company remembers. They claim that Operation has always been available; no one I know has seen it in years. Maybe it's making a comeback. Toy stores are heavily into nostalgia right now. Thanks to a couple of popular movies, many silly, old-fashioned amusements are now popular once again, like the Slinky, Mr. Potato Head, and Richard Nixon.

I gave the other game to a friend. He played it with his family, and then called me and said, "You know, that Operation game is pretty hard."

Smooth "Operation"

"What?" I asked him, incredulous. "You thought being a doctor was easy?"

While Operation is a game, it has some aspects that are just like real medicine. The patient, whose name is Cavity Sam, has twelve premade openings in his cardboard body. You "operate" on these areas of his anatomy, removing various comical body parts like "butterflies in the stomach" or "wrenched ankle."

This part is nothing like real surgery. There are no sharp instruments, and no bleeding. All you have is a pair of tweezers connected to a wire. If you slip, and the tweezers touch the metal edge of the opening, a loud rumbling noise comes out of Sam, and his red nose lights up like a traffic signal.

You start by drawing a card that tells you what part to remove, an easy diagnosis. The card also lists the fee, depending on degree of difficulty. ("The scores are in—that's a 7.4, an 8.1, and a 6 from the Russian doctor.") Also different from reality: you only get paid if the operation was a success. There are no points for trying.

When one of the regular "doctors" fails an operation, only then is a "specialist" assigned. Sam obviously belongs to an HMO. If successful, the specialist gets a higher fee, usually twice as much, for doing the exact same procedure. This is the part that is just like real life.

At the end, the winner is the one who has the most money. This bothers me. I think the object of the game should be to experience the gratification and fulfillment that comes from successfully removing a funny bone.

Being a real doctor, Operation should be a snap for me. It's not. Although I've been in operating rooms, I'm no surgeon. My five-year-old son routinely beats me. My friend was right—it is hard, especially those narrow openings for the "spare ribs" and "writer's cramp." Because of this, I can only play it where no one can see me, like alone in my basement at night.

Luckily, the worst thing that happens is when the nose lights up. So far, there is no companion game called Litigation, where people pretending to be lawyers take turns throwing the dice and suing you.

Are You a Real Doctor?

The game has been very popular around our house. I guess everyone loves to play doctor. In fact, the not-included batteries are already starting to wear out. My friend likes it, too. He's started giving me Operation tips. "OK, see, what you have to do is pinch the middle of the rubber band before you connect the knee bone to the ankle bone. . . ."

While it's not perfect, I'm sure there are other doctors who could use the game to brush up on their surgery skills. They might even want to use Operation for their continuing education credits, as long as they could play it in Hawaii.

Patients would benefit, too. They would see that being a doctor is not easy. I may buy a few more games for our waiting room, although if my patients got really good at it they might not need me. Maybe it will even spark someone's interest in becoming a doctor, although I seriously doubt it. In all the times I played Operation as a child, I never once thought I would someday perform one for real.

And judging by Sam's nose, that's probably a good thing.

Having the Sex Talk with Your Child

Our son went in for a checkup recently, and at the end of the appointment the doctor said it was time for us to talk to him about sex.

Right away there were two problems: (1) everything I know about this subject could easily have been covered during the fifteen-minute appointment, with enough time left over to explain complex polynomials, and (2) our son is only five years old.

This seems a little young to me. I was planning to do it the traditional way, avoiding this tricky subject until much later, like maybe prom night. At that point the designated parent, meaning the father, takes the child aside and, sweating profusely, mumbles something about birds, bees, cabbage patches, and waiting until you are old enough to pay for your powder blue tuxedo yourself.

This is wrong. Experts now say that the best time to talk to your kids about sex is before they start school. Young children are naturally curious about sex, just like they are curious about what happens when you put a jelly sandwich into the VCR and push fast-forward. Left on their own, they are bound to experiment, and that means you will come home one day to find them with the neighbor kids in the corner of the basement with a bunch of test tubes and a Bunsen burner.

If you never give them the facts, other kids will quickly fill in the gaps with the kind of weird, bizarre rumors about sex that children tell each other on the playground. Some of these stories, while anatomically impossible, are much more interesting than the truth, which can be—let's face it—kind of boring. Still, like Santa and the Easter bunny, fantasies like these only set them up for an eventual letdown. It's better for them to hear it from you, rather than have them show up on their wedding night with a bee hive and a bunch of cabbages.

Besides, these days you can't wait. Kids are exposed to sex at a much earlier age. Any child who watches TV is going to see actors pretending to have sex long before his or her parents get around to talking about it. Every year scientists count more than 2,000 references to sex on TV, and that's besides the "I had sex with my grandmother's alien houseplant" daytime talk shows. This is disturbing, because it means someone, somewhere is receiving federal grant money for watching TV, which most people do for free.

Sexual situations appear on TV almost as often as brutal murders. Actors on TV police dramas show their buttocks more than their badges. Family-hour sitcoms are loaded with off-color jokes, often recited by precocious child actors. Prime time soap operas show the same six characters having sex with each other on a rotating basis. If TV had been like this when we were kids we would have kept it hidden under the socks in the bottom dresser drawer.

So don't wait. Otherwise, you could end up like my friend, who was putting off having the sex talk until just the right moment. This turned out to be immediately after he caught his kids at the computer logged on to the gay and lesbian chat line.

Start talking about sex while your children are young, when it is easy. At this age, children do not need a lot of details. They don't want to know about zygotes and embryos and the independent assortment of DNA. They only want to know one thing: "Where do babies come from?" Once you tell them, they are more worried about how the baby is going to get out than how it got in there in the first place. Even the youngest child knows that fathers do something besides driving the car and buying more Huggies, but, luckily for parents, they don't particularly care what it is.

If they do, at least it's easier now than it used to be. In the old days, parents had only their own creativity, a couple of awkward hand motions, and lame metaphors referring to tadpoles and hard-boiled eggs. Now there are lots of reproductive resource materials for parents, including books, charts, and animated video tapes, which go way too far. Picture a flowing herd of happy, smiling sperm cells, and you'll see my point.

Of course, I plan to use several of these visual aids when I have my talk with my own son. This will help me achieve my main purpose—raising a happy, socially adjusted child, sure, but even more important, stretching things out to a full twenty minutes.

Dress Me Up, Dress Me Down

I don't worry about my clothes. Oh, I worry that they might bunch up and cause uncomfortable chafing, but I don't really think about the way they look.

This is because I have a serious fashion disability. I am congenitally unable to select clothing that is in style, or even that matches. Left on my own, I dress like a Polynesian islander just discovering the concept of plaid.

This can be a problem in medicine, a field where you are supposed to dress up. Everyone expects doctors to wear ties and nice suits, just like the doctors on *Chicago Hope.* My own role model was Doc on *The Love Boat,* who never even wore long pants.

Unfortunately, some people do not believe you are a real doctor unless you are dressed for the role. This never made sense to me. With a white coat on, the only clothes that show are the bottoms of my pants and a little triangle of white shirt near the neck. For all people know, I could be wearing a shirt dickey. Still, there are patients who take one look at my shoes and say, "All right, what have you done with the real doctor?"

Dress Me Up, Dress Me Down

It's just too bad I don't perform surgery, because then I could just spend the whole day wearing green surgical pajamas, just like I do at home.

To get around this problem I have always dressed in the classic conservative style, which means wearing the same clothes I wore in high school. This worked for years, with only one drawback: If I dressed like my grandfather now, what would I do when I got old?

Then I got married. For a long time my wife was willing to be seen with me. Then one day she started offering helpful suggestions about my wardrobe, such as, "For god's sake, when are you going to throw that away?"

This surprised me. While I was no GQ model, I was obviously dressing well enough to attract her as a mate. Now, for some reason, she wanted me to look better. "Look," I explained, "I am already married—I don't need to look nice." In case any men are nodding in agreement with that last statement, I must warn you that it is an extremely bad argument to use on your wife.

So I was forced to go shopping. I hate shopping for clothes. I can never find what I want, which is usually the same thing I have on. If I could, I would wear the same thing every day, just like a character in a comic strip.

Many men choose clothing based on qualities like durability and ease of replacement. It is a tragedy to find clothes you love, only to find out that they don't make them anymore. This happened with my favorite dress pants, Big Macs, which for years were sold in the husky indestructible synthetics section at JC Penney's.

Now stores are arranged by brand names, which means you have to know who designed a shirt before you can locate it. This is like coming home from camp with the wrong clothes that have someone else's name written in the collar.

Now the newest trend is "casual work" clothes, one of those terms like "jumbo shrimp" or "congressional leaders." To me, "casual" means baggy gym shorts and a torn "Irondale H.S." sweatshirt from a garage sale. This makes you dressed for work if your duties include the 600-yard dash.

In my fashion-impaired state, there was only one thing to do:

seek professional help. I turned myself over to the personal shopping service at a local department store. My case worker, a helpful woman named Amy, proceeded to dress me in various outfits like a life-sized Ken doll.

Using Amy's good taste where mine should have been in the first place, I was soon dressed in a fashionable sport coat and tie. I looked like a real doctor, meaning that I looked nothing like myself. Now when people refuse to believe I am a doctor, it won't be because of my clothing.

Of course, I only have the one outfit. Now I have to go shopping for some exact duplicate clothes, so I can look nice each and every day.

After all, I'm in the newspaper, too. Charlie Brown has been wearing that same yellow shirt with the zigzag stripe for over forty years, and if he can get away with it, so can I.

Real-Life Medical Revivals

There are people who say that medical shows on TV are not realistic, just because they treat life-and-death emergencies in a silly and sensational way.

Like the time on *Chicago Hope* when, during a crucial moment in transplant surgery, one of the nurses dropped the replacement heart on the floor. This kind of thing never really happens because, as any medical person can tell you, most major organs come equipped with safety straps.

Or the episode of *ER* when doctors were desperately trying to resuscitate a man having a heart attack. Things looked bleak until the janitor, who was doing some emergency mopping nearby, suddenly stepped forward, pushed the doctors aside, and performed life-saving open-heart surgery.

This particular janitor had been a cardiac surgeon in her own country, and was only doing maintenance work until receiving her U.S. medical license, which takes six to eight weeks for delivery. Hospital administrators were very grateful, especially after she cleaned up the mess and re-waxed the emergency room floor.

Are You a Real Doctor?

These life-and-death TV situations are not very realistic, mainly because they do not go far enough. Compared to some bizarre real-life emergencies, dropped hearts and scalpel-wielding janitors are nothing. Real emergency situations can be more ridiculous than anything on TV, including paid political advertisements.

Like the recent case in Oklahoma, where condemned murderer Robert Brecheen tried to commit suicide on the eve of his execution by taking an overdose of pills. Semi-alert prison guards rushed him to the hospital. There he was revived by a team of doctors and nurses, who were able to stabilize his condition until the next morning, when he was returned to prison and executed.

Clearly, the attitude of the prison system is, "You can't quit, you're fired." Through his suicide attempt Brecheen had cleverly managed to cheat death—for about two hours, the exact length of the TV movie about him, probably starring some guy from *Wings*. Once awake, he received his lethal injection, a more efficient overdose than he could manage on his own.

Lethal injections, because of important safety regulations, are always administered by doctors. After all, prison officials wouldn't want anything to go wrong. Otherwise the condemned might only lapse into a coma, which would require the expense of a second shot. I don't remember the entire Hippocratic oath, but I think this might violate the paragraph about killing people on purpose (the "Kevorkian clause"), even if a judge thinks they deserve it.

Still, there's no question—doctors are handy to have around in a pinch. Just ask Dr. Jean Cukier, a plastic surgeon who just happened to be in the right place to perform an emergency resuscitation on a plastic surgeon, Dr. Jean Cukier.

According to news reports, Dr. Cukier was fixing a lamp in his office when he accidentally shocked himself. This part is fairly realistic, given the handyman skills of many doctors. Immediately, he felt dizzy and noticed his heart beating rapidly, which led him to a quick and decisive diagnosis: he was in love.

If not, then he knew the shock had thrown his heart into an irregular rhythm. With the help of an assistant, Dr. Cukier hooked himself up to a cardiac beeping machine, which showed his heart beating like the drum solo in "Wipeout." Using every bit of his plastic surgeon know-how, he charged up the defibrillator paddles, tore off his shirt, and quickly gave himself a set of emergency breast implants.

No, actually, he somehow managed to shock himself with the defibrillator. This is an agonizing procedure, generally requiring powerful drugs to block the pain, or at least make patients forget who pushed the button. Shocking himself would have guaranteed Dr. Cukier a spot on the All-State Macho Self-Torture Squad, except for the fact that it didn't work. The current blasted him off the table and onto the floor, where he noticed several misplaced human hearts rolling around.

Fortunately, Dr. Cukier had the kind of "can do" attitude that doctors learn in medical school, where some of them take microbiology two or three times before passing. He climbed back onto the table and, despite the incredible pain, shocked himself again. This time it worked, and when the smoke had cleared he was able to do what he should have done in the first place: call the ambulance.

Weird stories like these prove that TV producers would be better off showing real-life emergencies instead of phony, made-up ones. With the new, looser standards at the FCC, this may happen. Soon all the major networks could be televising actual live emergency resuscitations—except at Fox, where they will show live nude resuscitations.

Just think, we might all get a chance to be on TV someday. I know what I will say when my turn comes: "Is there a janitor in the house?"

Moles—Should You Tell?

So, let's say it's summer time, you're a doctor, and you're riding your bike behind a young woman. As you pass you notice a mole on her shoulder. It's big, lumpy, and dark, with irregular borders that make it look like a tiny map of Wisconsin by night.

Like anyone, you would think, "That is probably a dysplastic compound nevus with atypia"—or, in plain talk, a scary mole. There is a pretty good chance that this ugly little splotch is a melanoma, the worst kind of skin cancer. Now for the hard part—do you say anything?

This happened to a friend of mine recently. During hot weather people tend to show more skin, which can be distracting to doctors who just can't stop themselves from examining it clinically. More exposed skin area means more chance of seeing something suspicious, which can lead to a difficult decision.

This is one of the classic doctor dilemmas, like trying to figure out if a lung collapsing in a forest makes any sound. Medical schools never teach you what to do—they are too busy making you

Moles—Should You Tell?

memorize the names of the various enzymes in saliva—but while doctors rarely discuss it, many of them have been in similar spots before.

Doctors feel funny about stuff like this, and not because they don't want to help people. Noticing a mole can be an invasion of privacy, especially when people realize they are being diagnosed without their knowledge or consent. Most doctors have a problem giving unwanted advice. Some worry that it looks like they are drumming up extra business for themselves.

Plus, there are sexual overtones to consider. My doctor wife, for example, would not hesitate to approach a woman with this problem. But a male physician might find himself facing hot pepper spray and uniformed police backup. Any diagnosis that takes longer than nine seconds might be considered ogling, which can, as we know, trigger bad feelings or, worse, a memo.

But melanoma is a deadly disease that can be recognized at a glance. Finding it early can mean the difference between a cure and a long, agonizing illness. And nothing else looks like a typical melanoma. There is very little chance that you will frighten and alarm someone because of a simple birthmark or smudge of dirt.

Not that speaking up is without risk. One time a dermatology resident in Philadelphia noticed an obvious cancer on the neck of the man riding in front of him on the bus. He suggested that the man might want to have the mole looked at. The man stood up and slugged him.

It doesn't always go badly. At a tennis exhibition some years ago, Rod Laver came out to meet the crowd, which happened to include several dermatology residents. They noticed a suspicious lesion on his cheek. Publicity photos on display also showed the spot, which was clearly growing larger over time. After nervous consultation, they decided to elect one person who would tell him to have it checked. They did, he did, a melanoma was removed, and Mr. Laver is still around today.

The lesson, clearly, is never to play tennis without a qualified skin specialist nearby. This is especially true today in the '90s, when so many moles are turning out to be cancer. This rise in melanoma, as most people know, has closely followed the increase in the amount of recurrent, unprotected exposure to Newt Gingrich.

Sunlight also plays a role. One in ten people today will develop melanoma, thanks in part to those of us who spent our college careers lying in the quad with a three-way mirror and Coppertone deep-frying oil. We thought tanning was healthy; now we know that sun transforms skin, first into beef jerky and later into malignant, precancerous cells.

My biking friend has been doing a survey of doctors, asking them how they would have reacted in his pedals. So far, the votes have been about three to one in favor of speaking up, with a few stray votes for notifying the police, sending an E-mail message, or saying something but only after first identifying yourself as famed dermatologist Newt Gingrich.

It's reassuring to know that most doctors would speak out. Still, when you ask actual people, as opposed to doctors, they universally vote 100 percent in favor of having a doctor say something, a clear mandate that the people want to know.

So protect yourself. Wear sunscreen, get a goofy hat, avoid C-Span, and maybe you won't ever feel that little tap on the shoulder that makes your knees start to shake and your stomach turn queasy. After all, it could be you-know-who.

Mud Slinging at the Health Spa

Before we get to today's subject, which is the health benefit of lying in a tub of putrefied mud, we must first ask the question: What is a health spa, and what makes it so healthy?

For me, the word "spa" conjures up images of Greek gods lounging around marble pools beside tall Ionic columns and clouds of volcanic steam, much like a Dockers commercial.

Instead, modern spas are simple retail outlets, often in minimalls, where you can receive a variety of bizarre cosmetic treatments. Dermatologists say that these treatments are of no value, but this is just not true—many of them are quite comical.

In one local health spa, according to their informative brochure, a person can spend hundreds of dollars on the face alone. This starts with a "cleansing facial" for $35, or perhaps a "clinical facial" for $50. This might seem confusing, but to a trained medical person the difference is obvious: $15.

They also offer "anti-free radical masks," a type of nuclear face lift. Free radicals are thought to cause cancer and, even worse, wrinkles. The treatments are designed to reduce them and "energize your skin," although any real change in free radicals would have to take place on a molecular level, which risks triggering cold fusion on your face.

Wacky treatments like these are touted as answers to premature aging, but this aging is rarely premature. Old people are supposed to have a few wrinkles. For some of them, premature aging is defined as "skin changes that become obvious while still having money to waste."

Most spas provide other services too. You can have a massage, or a variation like the chair massage, where your body is gently rubbed by folding kitchen furniture. They offer exfoliative body scrubs (called bathing by most people) and a variety of stress-relieving treatments, like having a stranger rub you all over with aromatic oils. I would find this fairly stressful.

Of course, it's hard to get the complete spa experience without including the ultimate worthless spa treatment—the mud bath. Luckily, I recently visited California, where mud baths are as common as trendy restaurants staffed by unemployed actors.

For journalistic accuracy, I must point out that I did not come in contact with any actual mud myself. While I believe in doing goofy things whenever you are in California—otherwise it's like going to Hershey, Pennsylvania, and not eating chocolate—on this particular trip I had already visited the beach where they film *Baywatch*, where I practiced holding in my stomach like David Hasselhoff for a full sixty minutes, excluding commercial breaks.

Instead, I accompanied a reliable source who was willing to submit to a mud bath. My source provided the research while I toured the facility and waited in the scenic parking lot.

The spa we chose had no Ionic or even Doric columns. It looked like a converted motel, with wrought iron railings and tasteless plastic vines. The setting was made even more cheesy by the sign outside: "Couples can enjoy a mud bath together in private treatment rooms."

While the standard mud bath treatment takes sixty minutes, only ten minutes are spent in the actual mud. It is, in fact, not mud at all, but a secret mixture of white clay, hot spring water, and peat moss, which is different from mud in the sense that it has more decayed vegetation. Essentially, it is like lying in a compost heap.

Unfortunately, you can't just jump in like you would into any other pile of rotting leaves. For one thing, the bottom of the tub is much too hot. You have to carefully lie on top of the mud and skoosh down into it, hanging there suspended like flotsam, or jetsam, or whichever is the proper term for a heavily soiled individual floating in muck.

The mud itself is also hot—very hot. This is supposed to "cleanse and purify" your body, while giving you the health benefits of making your heart beat like a cornered rabbit. Because you are naked, this superheated mud works its way into secret places you didn't know would hide mud, leaving little mud momentos that will still be turning up days later.

Mud baths are supposed to be detoxifying, drawing poisons and impurities from your body. I'm not sure what toxins they mean, but it does make you wonder who was in the mud bath before you. Hopefully, they took their toxins with them. There was no "sanitized for your protection" strip across the vat.

After ten minutes they pull you from the mud and hose you off, wrapping you up in a sheet like a take-out burrito. Finally you emerge, according to the brochure, "feeling renewed, rejuvenated, radiant, and refreshed," though muddy.

The health benefits of this are clear: there are none, which makes it a perfect addition for any spa. Even if there are no hot springs, most places have plenty of peat moss, and at least a few cheap motels. They can always have the plastic vines shipped in.

TV Doctor Shows Get Really Real

Considering how people hate going to emergency rooms, it's surprising that the TV show *ER* has become a huge smash hit.

This happened when people started talking about the show, which got it featured in every major magazine and newspaper, including in-flight magazines and obscure professional journals like *Current Endocrinology Review*. This incredible publicity did two things: (1) It made even more people tune in to see what the fuss was about, and (2) it allowed writers to use clever medical metaphors, calling the show "an IV adrenaline rush that resuscitates the entire doctor show genre, its popularity spreading like a flesh-eating bacteria that leaves the competition in critical condition."

The articles praise the hard-hitting realism, the rapid-fire pacing, the jumbled, overlapping story lines, and the constantly moving camera that makes viewers nauseous, letting them know what it feels like to be a patient. They also love the medical gobbledygook used by the actors, who are coached by real doctors and nurses to recreate the gritty, realistic feel of an actual medical facility, where nobody knows what anybody is saying. The publicity quickly reached the point where there are reports on news programs showing groups of doctors watching *ER* and commenting on how real it is.

How real is it? During the first episode the head nurse overdosed on drugs and died, only it was later changed to a coma. Now she is back, with hair that looks just great. During one episode a car pulled into the emergency room—literally. The doctors swept aside broken glass and stitched up the driver. One doctor usually gets drunk on nights when he is not delivering needed medicine to poor children. So far, none of the characters has had an evil twin, but I wouldn't bet against it.

Obviously, doctor shows are hot again, and I'm not going to miss my chance. Sure, not all doctors work in emergency rooms, but medicine is exciting and dramatic anyway, as shown in this exciting segment from "Suburban Clinic," my idea for a thrilling new, really real, TV doctor series:

> Theme music. Fade in on young, idealistic Dr. Clark Paulson as he struggles to help a woman with a bad skin rash. Carefully examining her upper back, he finally locates one large purple blemish and demonstrates the proper way to apply cortisone cream.
>
> Cut to: beautiful Nurse Debbie as she greets patients, her pleasant smile hiding deep, alarming doubts about her ability to juggle family and a nursing career while giving flu shots to thirty waiting patients.
>
> Meanwhile, young "Doctor" Brad, a promising but naive medical student, begins his first day in the clinic, where he is assigned the thankless job of removing ear wax from an elderly man who refuses to remove his cowboy hat.
>
> Cut to: Dr. Paulson, finishing a well-child exam. Shots are needed. He quickly calls the nurses, who are busy giving flu shots: "Quick, get this child a DTP, MMR, HIB, and HEP B stat, along with an adhesive strip of perforated plastic with cotton gauze and colorful drawings of a car-

toon beagle." All the nurses charge into the room, pushing a red cart with enough electronic equipment to track orbiting spacecraft.

All except Nurse Debbie, who is worried when her daughter is late from school. Rapid-fire, intercutting scenes show her daughter lost in a snowstorm, being held hostage by international terrorists, and as a passenger in a falling airliner. This causes her to bite her lower lip and quiver, making it difficult to give the next forty flu shots.

Cut to: an angry patient confronting Dr. Paulson, waving several insurance forms and threatening to stay until he fills them out. Security is called; a helpful guard shows the patient how to file forms correctly before walking him out past—

"Doctor" Brad, having trouble removing the wax. He begins to question his dedication, wondering if he was right to go into medicine to be able to wear white in any season. He wonders what grade he will receive from—

Dr. Paulson, now working on a large neck cyst. In an intense and powerful scene, he operates, knowing that any mistake will force the patient to wear his shirt collars buttoned up for weeks. The operation successful, he moves on to—

A patient who came for a sprained ankle, but who actually has a fracture. In a dramatic and moving scene, Dr. Paulson reveals the heart-rending truth, while promising to make him the best darn cast ever, in his choice of colors.

Meanwhile, several hundred more people storm the clinic demanding flu shots, pushing ahead of them Debbie's daughter, who is late from clarinet lessons. Debbie and the other nurses finally regain control of the unruly mob with an impassioned reading of flu vaccine indications and precautions from the P.D.R.

Cut to: young "Doctor" Brad, now completely frustrated, throwing the ear syringe away and vowing to become a mortgage banker when the patient suddenly says, "Wait a minute—I think I felt something move," and places his cowboy hat on Brad's head. Tears in his eyes, Brad returns to ear cleaning.

Touching theme music swells as we cut to Dr. Paulson, exhausted by a full day of saving lives, collapsing on his desk near a photo of his family.

Cut to: family members making preparations for Paulson's gala surprise birthday party. We fade out on the doctor's tired but satisfied expression, which does not change as the nurses sneak into the office and give him a flu shot. Fade out.

Women's Shoes: The Fashionable Menace

Now that more women are going into medicine, it is just a matter of time before they deal with one of the most serious threats to female health and well-being: women's shoes.

With medicine making exciting breakthroughs in DNA sequencing and visualizing actual brain activity, some people wonder why doctors would spend time worrying about shoes. The answer is simple: everyone has feet. Judging by the incredible amount of O. J. trial coverage, the same is not true of brain activity.

Foot pain bothers everyone at some point, and a lot of it is caused by women's shoes. (In men, this is obviously a symptom of a much deeper problem.) Women's shoes have been torturing and abusing their wearers for years. In a recent survey of healthy women, over more than 80 percent complained of toe pain and deformity caused by their shoes. Over half of them had bunions, which are not a snack item but a term for painful degeneration of the big toe, eventually causing it to line up sideways like a teenager trying to parallel park.

This is because women's shoes are too small. They are much too narrow, and they end in pointed triangles, which is not the original shape of anyone's feet. It is impossible to put five toes from a healthy, full-sized woman into a space the size of a Doritos-brand snack chip.

Despite the pain, women continue to wear them for one reason: fashion. (Men do other stupid things to cause themselves pain—see Hair Transplants; Softball Tournaments.) For some reason, it is fashionable for women to try to make their feet seem smaller. This is evidently some sort of turn-on for men, judging by the hundreds of personals ads desperately searching for SWF (small withered feet).

Most people don't realize that their feet get bigger as they get older. They never use those metal slide-rule foot gauges found in shoe stores, probably because they look like some sort of live-hold traps. Instead, they just keep buying the same size shoes they wore in high school, which fit about as well as other clothing from the period.

To illustrate my point, try this simple experiment: take five Lil' Smokies-brand mini-sausages and push them into the toe of an average pointy, high-heeled women's shoe. (Normally I would recommend Lil' Smokies Lite, which contain less fat, but for this experiment any small uncooked sausage product will do.) With all five Smokies in place, begin to exert downward pressure into the toe of the shoe using a kitchen mallet or other blunt object. One fact will be immediately clear: No one will ever want to wear this shoe again, and this is for the best.

High heels make the problem even worse. They tip the foot forward, forcing women to walk on their toenails and further compressing the poor toes, shoving them even deeper into the Bermuda Triangle of pointy footwear. Wearing high heels is like balancing your entire body weight on a couple of pencils, a very unstable situation. As a doctor, I have treated ankle fractures in women who fell off their shoes. These senseless, fashion-related injuries are one of the leading causes of ankle trauma, if you don't count stairways, all sports, and teenagers who leave their enormous shoes untied with the laces trailing several yards behind them.

To avoid these problems, women would be much better off wearing shoes of the proper size that are flat, roomy, and supportive—basically, ugly shoes.

The problem is where to find them. Shoe stores never display them in the front window, next to the snakeskin stiletto heels. They keep them in the back by the prosthetic limbs. I would not know where to look because, like many men, I never buy shoes. I already own a pair, which I will wear until they fall apart or I die, at which point someone will buy me new ones for the funeral.

Fortunately, women know where to look. They are constantly shopping for shoes. They have hundreds of pairs, even though they have the same number of feet as men. They will sometimes—and I know this is true—buy new shoes while the last ones are still in the box. The oldest, cast-off shoes are then moved to that ancient shoe burial ground, the back of the closet. Archeologists believe that backs of closets might hold thousands of women's shoes, which will only be discovered years later by the next owners of the house.

Luckily, they will probably never try to wear them, especially when they look inside and notice five small, disgusting lumps that might once have been mini-sausages. Like I said, it's for the best.

Coffee Is Hot

Coffee was the subject of a recent eye-opening report, warning all of us to wake up and smell the research.

The study, done by the National Research Institute for Things Everybody Already Knows, focused on the effects of caffeine. By using the important research tool of staying up late, scientists were able to prove that caffeine is clearly addictive.

"Addictive" in this case means difficult to do without, something that would never occur to most coffee drinkers. While the word is scary, the results were not. Subjects in the study who were deprived of caffeine were scientifically proven to go to bed earlier. None of them started breaking into houses and stealing VCR's to get money for Colombian dark roast, although one of them did cancel her child's birthday party because she was feeling a bit tired.

More importantly to regular users, being addicted to coffee can mean that it takes more and more of the stuff to get the same effects. This explains why gourmet coffee shoppes have been popping up on every corner like 7-Elevens.

Java, mocha, espresso, Joe—whatever you call it, coffee is hot. People now go to coffee shoppes like they used to go to bars, proving that this is a generation that would rather be wired than impaired. Instead of stumbling on the curb as they leave they can often sprint home.

These shoppes all have elaborate menus of various trendy coffee beverages, listing about thirty different names of drinks that are all basically coffee with varying amounts of milk. Instruction pamphlets and elaborate charts tell you the ingredients of each drink, how it was brewed, and an estimate of when the effects will wear off.

Those effects are simple: caffeine is a powerful stimulant for the entire body, especially the part responsible for taking an unconscious, wrinkled mass of twisted bed sheets and matted hair and converting it into something resembling human form. I like to think of myself as the kind of guy who can face the day on his own, without artificial stimulants. Unfortunately, there is absolutely no evidence that this is true, particularly since many of my neurons begin to fire only after a second cup. Coffee is the lever that we use to pry us out of bed and into daily life, and a lot of us wouldn't think of doing without it.

After those first few cups, though, caffeine can turn on you. Once you are already awake, caffeine can only make you even more awake, making you act like a jittery video tape of yourself played on fast-forward. Caffeine also affects your heart, causing the same response as vigorous exercise or having a bee fly up your pants leg. Having two cups of any espresso coffee drink gives you the warm, inner glow of knowing you have a major exam in the morning and can't find your notes. More and you feel like you are going 110 miles an hour in a Yugo, a conveyance never meant for that kind of speed.

There are times when this feeling can come in handy. Meetings, lectures, even writing—people are sometimes a lot more productive during this hyper-awake phase, although if you go too far your words! start! to! come! out! looking! like! this!

At other times it can lead to trouble. Caffeine accentuates the natural division between mind and body, making it possible to be wide awake physically while a mental vegetable. This is not the best way to perform major surgery, pilot the Concorde, or meet your new in-laws.

This is why they invented decaf. Scientists long ago developed a way to remove caffeine from coffee beans, possibly by sucking on them ahead of time. This produces decaf, which is the coffee equivalent of nonalcoholic beer and every bit as popular. With decaf, people can enjoy many popular espresso drinks without all the pesky side effects of caffeine. They don't, but they could. After all, what's the point? While you could theoretically drink large amounts of coffee and still get to sleep, as opposed to lying in bed with small electric generators attached to your limbs, the challenge would be gone.

Luckily, there is more to coffee than just caffeine. Otherwise people would be going to shoppes named after deer that serve only Jolt cola and No-Doz. Even decaf coffee has plenty of other results, like chronic stomach irritation and a strong diuretic effect.

Fortunately, the research showed that coffee, even a lot of coffee, won't lead to any serious health problems. While it may be addictive, coffee poses no long-term threat to your health. So except for banging your toe when you get up to pee, there is nothing to worry about.

So after all the fuss, the best advice about caffeine is what your mom would tell you, after conducting her own extensive research: some is OK, but too much is bad.

Big deal. That advice and a dollar will get you a cup of—well, maybe a nice milkshake instead.

Old TV Stars? Book 'Em

The Brady Bunch was for a while the number one movie in the country. I blame Dave Barry.

As most people know, Dave Barry is the syndicated columnist from Miami who is widely recognized by regular people and Pulitzer committees as the funniest human in the Western Hemisphere—and, with many former Eastern block countries now reporting in, maybe the world. More than 400 papers carry his column, and he has written over a dozen hilarious, best-selling books.

Dave Barry has been so successful, in fact, that his columns have spawned the TV sitcom *Dave's World*. The show is based on his life. Being television, a few small changes were made, like doubling the number of his children and making his jokes less funny.

Once a writer became a character on a hit TV show, some other TV characters started to believe they could be writers. This triggered a wave of books by popular TV sitcom stars. Their books now line shelves at bookstores everywhere, even the ones that carry greeting cards and tiny porcelain cats. Looking at a best-seller display today is like scanning cable channels at home.

Old TV Stars? Book 'Em

Many of these stars are former stand-up comedians who have been snapped up by Hollywood, where they build a show, and then a book, around their act. Jerry Seinfeld was first, followed by books from Tim Allen and Paul Reiser, several alternate versions of Roseanne's biography, and books by Ellen Degeneres, Brett Butler, Bill Maher, and Jeff Foxworthy. While not actually books in the sense of having plots or structure, they are often very funny, and several have become multi-million best-sellers. The authors then go on TV and read from the books, which are essentially stand-up comedy routines in convenient book form, and the cycle is complete.

Naturally, a lot of has-been, washed-up former TV stars were jealous. Even though no longer on TV, many of them quickly wrote books of their own, taking time out from their busy careers attending supermarket openings and drug rehabilitation programs.

This led to the book *Growing Up Brady*, by Barry Williams, who played Greg on the original *Brady Bunch*. Here he revealed that he had dated other members of the cast, including his TV sister, mother, several gaffers, and the guy who did the catering.

David Cassidy from *The Partridge Family* also wrote about life on the show. He couldn't date his TV mom because she was his actual real-life step-mom, something which would be too slimy even for a sitcom (*Leave It to Oedipus*, or maybe *Mr. Oed.*)

Soon there were books by all the surviving castaways of *Gilligan's Island*. (Both *Gilligan* and *Brady Bunch* were created by Sherwood Schwartz, who has a master's degree in biochemistry. This accounts for the subtle, carbon-based organic subtext that runs through both shows.) These include memoirs from Gilligan, the Professor, and Mary Ann, who wrote *The Gilligan's Island Cookbook*, or *101 Things to Do with Fiberglass Coconuts*.

And not just sitcoms, either. Adam West's *Back to the Batcave* tells us the real reason he looked so fat in the bat suit. (It was the utility belt, honest.) Dobie Gillis never got any appreciation for his work (Work!). William Shatner once had friends and real hair.

The success of these books made Hollywood take notice. Movie studios now give us high-budget, big screen reruns of old TV series like *The Beverly Hillbillies, Maverick, The Addam's Family,* and *The*

Fugitive. This led directly to *The Brady Bunch Movie,* which, during its run, was the leading cause of slowing heart rates in theater audiences (Brady-cardia syndrome).

With TV showing writers, bookstores becoming TV, and the movies turning into Nick at Night, the obvious question is: What's left for the current crop of movie stars? The logical answer is to turn these movie celebrities into writers.

Imagine a money management column from Kim Basinger, who gives practical advice on filing bankruptcy and creating full, pouty lips. Or "Dear Abby" written by human hairdo Julia Roberts (Abby says: "Um . . . gosh, that's . . . What was the question?"). "True Lies" would become a Washington affairs column by Arnold Schwarzenegger ("Senate democwats cheewed as ze bawanced budget amendment was demowished. Hasta la vista, baby."). And "News of the Weird" would be written by Jaye Davidson, star of *The Crying Game.*

I'm holding out for Kevin Costner for this column, even though I'll be lucky to end up with that chubby guy who tried to smuggle dinosaur embryos out of Jurassic Park. I'll be waiting by the phone, dreaming up wacky plots for a sitcom and trying to find a way to explain to my wife when my son's character, for important television reasons, is split in two.

High-Tech Cooling Trend

Just like anybody, I sometimes need advice from a qualified professional. The last thing I need is some cold, impersonal specialist babbling on in confusing scientific jargon about the latest high-tech scan or computerized tests.

As you have probably guessed, I'm talking about the weather reports on TV.

The weather has gotten much too technical. When I was a kid our weathermen were friendly people named Bud. They came on once a day just before the sports guys in the plaid jackets, and they basically told us whether or not it was raining. To demonstrate, they stuck little cartoon raindrops or smiley sunshine faces onto a colorful cardboard weather map. Even as a kid, I got it.

Weathermen have now been replaced by meteorologists, highly trained specialists in a field that didn't even exist yet at my high school career day. The cartoon maps have become aerial satellite photos, which show large patches of weather slowly spreading like a fungus across the Midwest. Some of them are so detailed that if you get up next to the screen and look carefully you can see yourself sitting in your house watching TV.

This incredible technology lets meteorologists know what kind of weather is coming in from North Dakota, saving them a phone call to Bismarck. They gesture at these maps, parts of their fingers disappearing into the blue background as they indicate the big picture: "Tomorrow's forecast calls for a large white line with pointy triangles, followed by intermittent wavy lines in the morning."

These reports come at six, nine, noon, five, six, and ten, besides hourly updates, reminders, and "Weather Minutes" to bring you up to date on last-minute developments. NASA doesn't need this kind of weather surveillance. Anyone getting this much weather news has no time to go outside.

Unfortunately, despite this incredible technology, modern weatherpersons still have trouble predicting the weather. Meteorology is not an exact science. At the very least, a meteorologist should be able to accurately predict when huge chunks of flaming rock will come falling out of the sky.

The truth is that even professional television meteorologists, many of them so dedicated that they have received painful hair transplants, will admit that they correctly predict rain about as often as a medium-sized bunion.

That's why they never give absolute predictions, only probabilities. According to meteorologists, a clear blue sky without a cloud in sight can have a 30 percent chance of rain. (I must be somehow weather-impaired, because I have no idea what these numbers mean. I guess I'm supposed to invite only 70 percent of the people to the picnic) Even during raging thunderstorms, the chance of rain never goes higher than about 80 percent. This is not a reassuring statistic when you are watching your patio furniture float off down the road.

They even hedge on these percentages, updating every fifteen minutes until the actual weather arrives: "Only 30 percent chance of rain, folks, so grab the kids and head out for a great—hold on, it's clouding up, make that 50 percent—Was that thunder? OK, 80 percent chance of rain today. Better get out those umbrellas."

Because rain gives them trouble, they talk instead about pressure.

High-Tech Cooling Trend

At any given moment there is a low-pressure system moving in, pushing ahead of it some higher pressure leading to a sudden drop in the barometer, which measures pressure. This is evidently useful information for deep sea divers and hot-air balloonists. Me, I never know how to dress for the pressure.

During severe weather, most stations interrupt their continual updates with even more intense weather coverage. These reports are always broadcast from so-called weather centers, special rooms containing more computer equipment than Starfleet Command. From there, using advanced computer graphics and scientific modeling techniques, they are able to broadcast bulletins that confuse everyone. Is it a watch or a warning? Which one is worse again? What if I don't have a transistor radio? Do I really have to go outside and lie in a ditch? It was easier when they just blew a siren and everyone went into the basement, except for the people falling off their garage roofs trying to get a look at the severe weather.

Not even other meteorologists know what to do for sure. In 1990, Hurricane Andrew literally blew the roof off the National Hurricane Forecasting Center in Coral Gables, Florida, and at the time the place was still full of meteorologists, who had evidently been listening to "classic rock" stations instead of their own warnings.

Luckily, that kind of dangerous weather is unusual. Most of the time, TV stations are really just spending millions of dollars and countless hours of air time in an ongoing effort to make sure that no one, God forbid, gets wet.

Because of my own personal meteorologically challenged state, I have had to come up with my own system. If I want to do something outside, I look out the window. There I generally find some weather. If it's raining, and I want to do something that I can't do while wet (fewer activities than you might believe), then I stay inside instead.

I think that's the way Bud would have wanted it.

Women Are from Venus, Menopause from Mars

The votes are in, and its official: once again, the number one most prescribed medicine in America is estrogen, the female hormone taken by women after menopause. The entire country is in the grip of a gigantic hormone surge as strong as anything that affected us in junior high school.

This is surprising, because estrogen is not an easy medicine to prescribe. It's not like giving penicillin for strep throat. Estrogen has so many effects and side effects that patients and even doctors can easily get confused. This is why half of those prescriptions are never filled or thrown away during the first year.

There are some doctors, many of them men, who believe every woman over fifty should take daily estrogen for life. This suggests a major design flaw in female human physiology. It's hard to imagine that half the population requires an expensive daily prescription medicine just to be normal.

Other doctors, many of them women, think that menopause is a natural phase of life. To them, menopause is not a disease, and does not require treatment, thank you very much.

Whenever therapy is controversial, the best thing doctors and patients can do is review the evidence and decide together on the best choice:

On one hand, estrogen does protect women from heart disease. Some studies show that women taking estrogen live longer, with a lower chance of having heart attacks.

On the other hand, it increases the risk of endometrial cancer inside the uterus. This means most women have to take a second drug, progesterone, to prevent the lining from building up. Unfortunately, progesterone seems to nullify estrogen's protective effect on the heart. Plus, it means most women will start having periods again, and you can imagine how popular this is.

On one hand, estrogen prevents osteoporosis, the loss of calcium and other minerals that makes bones brittle and causes hip fractures in older women.

On the other hand, it may cause an increase in breast cancer. Nobody knows for sure. Last year, reports in the top two leading medical journals published one month apart looked at this relationship, and they came up with exactly opposite conclusions. Even the possibility is enough to keep women away from the doctor's office, for fear someone will bring it up.

On one hand, estrogen does get rid of the hot flashes that come during "the change."

On the other hand, Premarin, the most widely used form of estrogen, is made from the urine of pregnant horses. (PREgnant MARes, get it?) These horses are kept chained in tiny pens, and their infant foals are taken from them and slaughtered so they can be quickly impregnated again.

Altogether, that comes to six hands, more than a patient and a doctor have between them. This means that people should also consider the evidence from other, different sources and decide for themselves. For example, after reviewing the available literature about estrogen and its side effects, I have decided not to take it.

Of course, as you can see from the photo, I'm a man (yes, I am). What do I know? The symptoms of menopause in men—buying sports cars, dating teenagers, getting hair transplants—are not related to estrogen, but to stupidity.

Women have it much harder. Every month they are bombarded with articles in newspapers and magazines that give insightful, probing looks at these drugs. Like prestigious medical journals, they often contradict articles from the month before.

Well, I'm not going to get in the middle of this. My job, both at the newspaper and in the little exam room, is to present the facts in clear, easily understandable language that outlines the options while avoiding hate mail from women's groups or drug companies.

Once armed with the facts, each woman can decide for herself whether the risks of estrogen are worth the possible benefits. It's like having Clint Eastwood as your doctor: "Ma'am, ask yourself—how lucky do you feel?"

If the answer is, "Not very," then there are alternatives. Exercise and eating right do as much to prevent heart attacks as estrogen. Hot flashes are terrible, but they go away. Calcium supplements can prevent fragile bones, especially if you start when you are young.

Believe it or not, some of the women who do these things are actually relieved when they reach menopause. At that point they can finally put their troublesome hormones behind them and focus on other things. After all, it's been a long time since junior high.

Power Rangers— Yes or No?

As a doctor, parents are always asking me important medical questions about raising children, like whether to let them watch Mighty Morphin Power Rangers on TV.

To anyone who knows me, one thing is clear: Boy, are they asking the wrong person. I generally love stuff like this. I believe that children need fantasy, just as they need the security of knowing good will always triumph over evil. (Later they can learn about war, famine, and the House of Representatives.) The idea of a team of super-powered teenagers recruited by an all-knowing computer intelligence to battle the forces of evil and save our planet from destruction—well, it works for me. When patients bring in their Power Ranger action figures I usually end up playing with them myself. Sometimes I whine and pester their moms to buy new ones for next time.

Power Rangers have become more popular than Batman Cabbage Patch Barbie Super Squirter Ninja Turtles. Even kids who never watch TV come home singing "Go, Go, Power Rangers," picking it up via osmosis from the air waves. According to costume sales projections, on Halloween night the sidewalks will be jammed with kids dressed as their favorite Power Ranger, meaning the red one, or, in particularly creative and independent children, the green one. Ranger costumes will be worn by three out of four kids and, in a few sad cases, their parents.

There is more to a television show, however, than just colorful costumes and superpowers. To make any recommendations you need to evaluate the show based on its performance in several crucial areas, as shown in this handy list:

Political Correctness

PRO: Current cast includes several ethnic and racial types, unlike original version which featured only Japanese actors inside official Power Ranger helmets ($24.95 at toy stores).

CON: Roles are stereotypes, with the Asian girl becoming the yellow Ranger, the African American the black, and the air-headed fashion-slave valley girl, pink.

Gender Equality

PRO: Here in America, two of the rangers, fully 40 percent, are female. (In Japan, at the risk of causing a major gender identification crisis in pre-schoolers, the yellow Ranger is a boy.)

CON: Clearly the wimpy rangers, the ones generally held hostage by evil alien beings.

Physical Science

PRO: High-tech machines and communication devices which are never explained, just like real life.

CON: Distorted sense of spatial relationships when evil space aliens suddenly and for no apparent reason grow to the size of the Eiffel Tower. This allows Power Rangers to assemble into gigantic Mega-Zord and do battle amongst the skyscrapers, as if there were skyscrapers in a place called Angel Grove.

Academic Achievement

PRO: All excellent students, the best in the school.
CON: That's because their school is full of complete idiots with names like Bulk, who each episode falls down with his face in a cake.

Multiculturalism

PRO: Much of Ranger footage is actually Japanese, allowing viewers to appreciate flavor of another culture.
CON: Full-face helmets hide amusing lip-synching mistakes like in Godzilla movies.

Moral Standards

PRO: Episodes often have a moral, presenting a rudimentary value system.
CON: Message often distorted by bizarre context, for example: "Don't be jealous of a friend, or you might be imprisoned forever in another dimension by a hideous orchid monster created by an evil alien overlord."

Violence Prevention

PRO: Features anti-violence message at the end of some episodes.
CON: Comes after twenty-two minutes of mindless kung fu kicking.

This is the real problem with the show. If anything, the Rangers aren't super enough. Their only superpower seems to be kicking people, a distinction that would even make a superhero out of Steven Seagal ("The Adventures of Puffy-Faced Pony-Tail Man"). As any daycare provider can tell you, this kind of thing rubs off. In fact, controlled research studies show an increase in kicking among psychology graduate students after only one or two episodes.

Are You a Real Doctor?

Even worse, when kicking isn't enough, they turn to weapons. Rangers carry guns at their sides, like characters in an old Western. There is no imagination or fantasy in pulling a gun. We can see that any evening on the news.

Because of this, some parenting experts say that Power Rangers have no place in a child's world. Sure, and I suppose they would also say there are no space aliens standing ready to ravage our planet and destroy our way of life. This is the kind of thinking that got the Power Rangers banned in Norway, where they blame their problems on violent American shows that are made in Japan.

The colorful costumes, the fantasy, the teamwork, the happy endings—we can all learn a lot from the Power Rangers. Unfortunately, it won't all be good. Remember, children have trouble sorting out TV fantasy from reality, whereas adults generally know what will happen if they try to fly from the top of the playground slide.

Should your children watch Power Rangers? I guess it depends on whether you want to get kicked. Even if you don't, your kids can still wear the costumes, sing the song, and play with the action figures. They'll use them to make up their own Power Rangers stories. As a bonus, they won't be exposed to thirty-eight obnoxious commercials in every half hour of kid's television.

On the other hand, should you watch them yourself? Absolutely. And don't forget your costume—Halloween will be here again before you know it.

Home Healing

I am constantly amazed by the way the human body can heal itself, especially since my car can't.

Or won't. I've always suspected that cars could secretly fix themselves if they wanted to. I always give them a few weeks whenever I hear some new sound coming from under the hood, but it never works. Sometime before leaving the factory they are brainwashed by teams of car mechanics, who convince them to stay broken until they get back to the shop, where they are treated to high-quality motor oil and free rides on the lift.

I have better luck with other inanimate objects like houses. There are roughly 6 x 10⁸ things that can go wrong with a house. Many of them happen during the first six months, as the ink is drying on the mortgage. Most new home owners get discouraged when they are faced with a loose window frame or a dryer that makes clothes wetter, but luckily, I am a trained medical professional. I have experience in diagnosing and treating many simple problems, although usually in human beings. Still, when something goes wrong in our house I use the same methodical approach I learned in medical school.

First, I take a complete history. This generally means asking my wife when she first noticed the problem. Wives are always the ones who notice these things, although I am not accusing her or anything. I think they may be just more attentive to things like loose bathroom towel racks or light switches that shoot sparks.

The next step is to carefully examine the problem area. This is important, even if it ends up making things worse. Grabbing the towel rack and giving it a good shake will produce a shower of little pieces of plaster and make the rack even looser, but it also gives me valuable insight into the scope of the problem.

With this data, I can then make my assessment: "There's nothing wrong with it," I tell my wife.

Oddly enough, she rarely accepts this conclusion, even though it is clearly based on a scientific analysis of the data at hand. Instead, she seems strangely focused on "doing" something.

"Maybe we should fix it," she will suggest helpfully, using a special tone of voice that clearly means for me to fix it.

Now, in a delicate situation like this, the last thing I want to do is charge in with a bunch of power tools. Don't get me wrong—I'm a male-type person. I possess the gene for power tool usage. I've been to the hardware store and back. I have my own power saw, which I keep locked in a basement cabinet with the blade off. I could easily jump in, making a noise like an F-15 taking off and raising a cloud of plaster dust big enough to block out the sun.

But here's the actual truth: I know a lot of these little things will fix themselves. I have seen it happen. A loose rack can often become tighter if you just wait for a while.

I'm not exactly sure how this happens. The older guys at the hardware store call it "framing settle ground heave," or something like that. "A house can shift on you," they say, nodding knowingly. This explains why my driveway gets a little longer each winter during shoveling season.

Knowing this principle, I usually fall back on standard orthopedic theory: All I have to do is keep the two broken pieces close together and hold them fairly still while nature does the rest.

In this particular case, the towel rack is in a good position, right up against the desired place in the wall, and all that is needed is a little distraction—not on the individual pieces, but on my wife.

"Can't be done," I tell her. "Do we have any lighter towels?"

As I mentioned, this is not the first thing ever to go wrong in our house. "That's OK," she says, smiling and patting my shoulder. "I'll just call someone to take a look at it. . . ."

At this point, a wave of fear runs through me, and I am forced to abandon science, throwing seven years of advanced medical training right out the window. I know that any handyman would be happy to consult on the case of the loose towel rack, charging only slightly more than it would cost for exploratory neurosurgery.

Soon I'm back at the hardware store, asking the old guys what to do. "Why didn't you say so?" they tell me, trying not to laugh. "Here, what you need is some Quik-Drying Acrylic Towel Rack Plaster Fixator. Just put a tube in your reversing pneumatic pressure applicator and—you have one of those, don't you?"

Several hundred dollars later I am back home with a scribbled list of instructions. While I have faith in the hardware guys, I also know that this list is really to keep me busy until enough time has passed for the rack to heal itself back onto the wall.

So I carefully follow the instructions, and in less time than it takes to create a new system of government, our towels are once again securely on the wall where they belong.

"Oh," my wife says, feigning surprise, "What a good handyman you are. Nice job."

"Don't be silly," I tell her modestly. "It's just diagnosis and treatment, like I do every day." I smile back, giving her a hug and trying hard not to think about the little grinding sound I heard coming from the transmission on the way home.

Closing In on Jargon

I am tired of people saying that doctors can't speak English. This is just not true. Many of them know how to speak English perfectly well, they simply choose not to.

Most doctors were once fluent in the English language, sometime way back before medical school. Now they rely instead on a strange combination of English and medical jargon, a sort of "Mediglish." It consists of short English phrases and conjunctions, interspersed with obscure, pretentious medical terms.

This is the language spoken in most modern health facilities, a fact which drives patients crazy. They often have no idea what doctors are talking about. A doctor may be merely reporting the latest lab results, but somehow the patients think they will soon be losing a couple of vital organs. Patients and their families would have a better chance of understanding the language if they randomly parachuted into some eastern European country.

Still, it bothers me when people make fun of doctors. A lot of professions have their own language, made up of obscure terms and

Closing In on Jargon

confusing jargon that nobody else understands. To prove it to yourself, try this simple experiment: refinance your house.

My wife and I did this recently, and we learned that the finance community also has its own language, which it uses to make buying and selling houses seem like advanced theoretical nuclear physics.

Basically, buying a house means signing your name to thousands of pieces of paper, all of them unreadable. The process takes several weeks, requiring many phone calls that are not returned. At some point you manage to reach the secret specified number of papers, making you eligible to move on to the actual closing ceremony, a sort of lightning round for refinancing.

My wife and I arrived at this event armed with our checkbook and several of our own pens, in an effort to show we really knew our way around the real estate game.

The ceremony itself is quite exacting. It involves sliding pieces of paper across the table in a very specific order, where you sign them and slide them back. The process is so complex, in fact, that there is an entire job devoted to sliding pieces of paper in front of you and pointing to dotted lines. It is called the closer, but only because no one wants to be referred to as a mindless paper slider.

At some random point in every closing ceremony, the closer will suddenly call a foul. This puts the entire transaction on hold until you are able to produce, say, notarized evidence that you once worked for a large multinational corporation (McDonald's) while still in high school. If you cannot produce the required papers, the closer is authorized to accept a large amount of cash, just in case.

This happened to us. We were doing our best to keep up, signing our names everywhere and smoothly switching pens when they ran out of ink, when our closer suddenly brought things to a screeching halt, citing several important points of imaginary real estate law. "I'm sorry, but the settlement title abstract has to be prorated," she said, shuffling papers quickly to distract us.

Keep in mind what was happening here: We were buying our own house, from ourselves, and selling it right back to us. This should have been easy, especially since we had already agreed on a price.

I admit that I got a little flustered. While I understand medical jargon, I'm not used to dealing with somebody else's pointless gibberish. I quickly fell into the only defense I could come up with: I started talking gibberish right back to her.

"Well, ascending cholangitis can be ameliorated through parenteral antibiotic therapy," I replied.

She eyed me carefully. "Of course, personal mortgage insurance is required for any transaction involving a federally approved lender."

"Retrograde pyelography," I nodded. "Otherwise, ureteral reflux will result in deterioration of the renal parenchyma."

"Long-term deferred annuities."

"Subacute bacterial endocarditis."

At this point we were at an impasse, although I felt she was clearly losing her cool. Her neat little piles of paper had started to fan out on the table. In desperation, she suddenly blurted out a statement which, to the best of my recollection, sounded exactly like this: "The borrower's compliance disbursal of funds is entirely contingent upon certification of occupancy of the settlement statement for initial escrow account, providing prepayment."

Looking back, I know I probably went too far, but she had made me mad. On top of everything, I hate signing my name.

"You know, I couldn't help noticing that mole on your neck," I said casually. "It's probably nothing, but I think you should have it checked. It could be a CONGENITAL SUB-DERMAL DYSPLASTIC JUNCTIONAL NEVUS."

I'm not sure what happened afterward. We still live in the same house. So far, nobody has showed up at the door with a bunch of their own stuff, so I assume things went OK. My wife remembers signing a paper that promised the closer free dermatologic care for life, but I am not sure—it's just so hard to understand jargon, you know?

Fun at the Casino? Don't Bet on It

"Only One Mile To Fun," reads the road sign at the entrance to our local casino. My friend Doug and I have seen these signs every few miles, warning us that we were closing in on fun in case we were allergic and needed to take precautions. The parking lot is not full, but only because it is the size of several megamalls, with half the spots taken up by buses. We walk in, two middle-aged guys with ten dollars and a hankering for fun.

$10

Inside, we watch a free show featuring a big-name comedian performing in what could be a school lunch room, with long narrow tables and hall monitors that sell drinks. The show might be fun except for the noxious clouds of cigarette fumes and the people behind us, who evidently feel comedy is a participation event and talk loudly the entire time. A glass of pop costs us a quarter, thanks to a common casino time-warp effect that makes any food cost the same as in 1965.

$9.75

Searching for fun, we walk through a long building like a bowling alley decorated in early kilowatt. There are colored lights on every vertical surface. Everywhere are rows of slot machines, their shiny faces flashing like highway warning signs. Even on a Tuesday evening, more than half of the stools are occupied by elderly men and women holding Big Gulp containers full of coins. We select a machine, the roving change waitress turns the rest of our money into quarters, and we start to play.

$8.75

We drop in four quarters, pulling the handle each time. Most people near us just push the "play" button instead, keeping physical movement to a minimum and avoiding pesky repetitive motion injuries. They stare ahead, trance-like, as the wheels click to a stop. Then they push the button again.

$8.25

After a few more coins we continue our quest, cruising through the various gaming rooms. Each room has several blackjack tables in the center, manned by dealers wearing bow ties and Dairy Queen uniforms. Unlike the casinos in James Bond movies, there are no debonair British men wearing tuxedos. Many of them are wearing tractor hats instead. While almost everyone is smoking, there is not a single cigarette holder. Oddly enough, almost every table has a player with crutches. They seem to lose just as much as the others.

$7.50

We stop at another row of slot machines. Our third quarter wins

$1.50, but we have to push another button to get the machine to spit the coins into the metal tray. Normally, it will hold onto them for you, saving you the trouble of putting them right back in again. We put them right back in again, only this time nothing comes back out. We watch several other slot machine zombies lose what could well be their rent and insulin money. So far, we have seen no one having fun; in fact, we are starting to feel sad.

$6.75

Finally, a woman next to us hits the jackpot. She is using a casino card, not quarters, which rests in a slot at the top of the machine. The wheels click to a stop with all three pictures matching. The lights flash wildly, but the woman does not seem to notice. Staring ahead, she watches the screen as it totals up her winnings. It finally comes to a halt at $258. The machine credits her card while the woman stares blankly ahead, with no flicker of emotion on her face. After a few seconds, she reaches out and pushes the "play" button again, falling back into the same losing rhythm.

$6.25

Now clinically depressed, we give up. We are unable to find anyone having fun. The closest thing is when Doug finds a television showing the last two minutes of a Michigan State basketball game, saving himself three hours of watching the game on tape. The next time a departing nursing home tour group is announced, we leave with them.

$0

Driving home we stop at a fast-food drive-through window. The woman who takes our order is rushed and a little rude. We pay the entire bill in quarters, which is fun.

An Aspirin a Day Keeps the Cardiologist Away

Here's some news from the exciting field of cardiology: It's too late.

Anyone who needs a cardiologist is probably in trouble, especially if they need one at 3:00 A.M. This is because cardiologists take care of patients with heart disease, which most people try to avoid. I know many cardiologists, and I can tell you that they are smart, capable, caring physicians. Even so, you do not want to be their patient if you can help it.

At a recent conference on coronary care I was given a glimpse of the latest incredible, high-tech advances in the field. Heart attacks are usually caused by blocked arteries, and over the years cardiologists have developed many elaborate ways to reopen these blockages, including drilling them, dissolving them, bypassing them altogether, and propping them open with little balloons. While use of the balloon procedure is expanding, there has been no real change in the preferred method for treating heart disease, which is not to get it in the first place.

There are many things you can do. For example, doctors at this conference presented an exciting new report about a medicine that prevents heart attacks. This wonder drug can even reduce the chance of a second heart attack in people who already have cardiologists. It can even help stop a heart attack in progress. Best of all, this miracle medicine is something you probably already have in your medicine cabinet, next to the Sudafed and dental floss: it's aspirin.

This is like learning that Blistex cures cancer. Drug companies are always creating exotic new heart medicines, costing several dollars a pill, that are supposed to prevent heart attacks. When they do the research, however, the results always show that plain old aspirin, costing $1.89 for a hundred, does a better job. The drug companies, realizing that a cheaper, safer, more effective medicine is already available in supermarkets, then triple their budgets for magazine ads and promotional trinkets for doctors.

What this means is that someday you might experience crushing chest pain and be rushed via ambulance to the hospital, where highly trained ER doctors will quickly spring into action, handing you a paper cup of water and an aspirin tablet. This is not part of some cruel cutback in HMO coverage. It's just good medicine.

Aspirin is so effective that it should probably be used by anyone over forty. The official dose is a half tablet a day. For most people this means one whole tablet every day they remember, which comes down to the same thing. Baby aspirin can be used instead if you can open the plastic child-proof cap without breaking a tooth. Using aspirin is safe, easy, and effective. I put one in the gas tank of my car each day, just in case.

The other exciting new prevention therapy available in grocery stores is vitamin E. For the last few years, people have been speculating that certain vitamins might help prevent heart disease. Experts at the conference called this a promising breakthrough, except that it doesn't work.

The latest research does not prove that taking vitamin E pills prevents anything. In fact, anecdotal evidence suggests that it can be somewhat of an aphrodisiac, which can lead to increased sex drive resulting in certain types of strenuous exertion that place an extra load on the heart, and there you go.

Except in this scenario, increasing your vitamin intake is still a good idea, but only if you buy them in their natural packaging. This does not mean taking a pill, but eating a lot of fruits and vegetables.

These foods are very high in vitamins, besides having a lot of fiber, which is why experts recommend five servings a day. Many people don't even know that there are five different fruits, but they keep coming up with new ones, like kiwifruit, which, judging by the hair, is actually more of a pet.

There is a lot of research showing that this kind of diet pays off. Eating more natural food, low in fat and high in fiber, is 100 percent guaranteed to lower your risk of a heart attack. If nothing else, eating a lot of apples and carrots will take up room in the stomach that might otherwise be used for nachos and bean dip.

Which they never serve in coronary care units. This is just another reason to stay out of them. In most hospitals the CCU ward is a pleasant, well-lit area, nicely decorated with the latest in cardiac technology and staffed by friendly, competent nurses, but believe me, it's not the place to have a room of your own.

Where No Doctor Has Gone Before

Thirty years ago *Star Trek* first appeared on small, black-and-white TV screens across America. Since then it has spawned an entire entertainment industry. There have been three other TV series, eight movie sequels, and a mountain of *Star Trek* merchandise, from lunch boxes to NASA space shuttles. Several times a year, conventions of "Trekkers" bring together people from all walks of life, even physicians, to wear pointy foam-rubber ears and discuss the problems of the twenty-third century. They tell each other to "live long and prosper."

Before any of that, though, was *Star Trek,* the original TV show. Back then, in weekly episodes viewed by very few people, the Star Ship Enterprise first explored the vast reaches of space. Its captain and crew reached out to new planets and new civilizations, spreading the word that mankind had arrived and meant no harm. Not bad for people who never changed out of their bell-bottom pajamas.

Are You a Real Doctor?

Even as a young boy, one member of the crew was always my favorite: Dr. "Bones" McCoy, the ship's doctor, played by DeForest Kelly. Sharp and outspoken, his job was to protect the crew from the dangers of outer space. This involved much more than giving them flu shots. Almost every week, Dr. McCoy would face things like intelligent mutant bacteria from Galton-6, or shape-shifting weed people that survive on the salt content of human tissues. Each time he would find a way to protect the crew using the strange and powerful medical technology of the future. He was a great doctor.

Even under that kind of pressure, Dr. McCoy never wavered from his duty. He would step right in, wave a glowing flashbulb over his patient and come up with an instant diagnosis. Once the problem was clear, he would know immediately what had to be done, which was usually, "Get this man back to the ship right away." There were no secrets from Dr. McCoy, and his medical skills were as important to the security of the ship as the phaser guns, set on "stun," that hung from their belts. ("Body temperature is way too low, heart beat is all wrong, blood pressure—Jim, this man is a Klingon spy!")

The best thing about Dr. McCoy was that he knew his place on the Enterprise. He was a doctor, and nothing more. He would say so each time the captain asked him to perform some impossible miracle to save the crew. These heated exchanges were the best part of the old shows. I think of them all the time in my own practice.

"Dammit, Jim, I'm a doctor, not a politician." All Dr. McCoy wanted to do was take care of his crew. If that interfered with the culture or policies of an alien government, too bad. He was committed to his patients. I try to keep this attitude in mind when I deal with insurance companies.

"I'm a doctor, not a carpenter." In the future, doctors aren't used to worrying about simple problems like broken bones. Today, we treat fractures by holding the injured bones immobile long enough for the body to heal itself. They do the same thing in the future, but under the influence of magnetic field generators and osteoblastic stimulation, it takes about three minutes. I have to be more of a "carpenter" than Dr. McCoy, and I'll have to live with that until technology catches up with television.

"I'm a doctor, not a fortune teller." This was Dr. McCoy's response whenever the captain asked him for some prediction, like, "Bones, how long can they survive on the asteroid before they freeze to death?" or "Bones, how can this civilization reproduce if the men and women refuse to touch each other?" Dr. McCoy knew better than to give odds. He knew that predictions are difficult to make, and will almost always prove you wrong.

"I'm a doctor, not a mind reader." Despite two centuries of progress, the crew of the Enterprise is no different than people in our time. They always assume that a doctor can tell what someone else is thinking. It is not true today, and it will not be true in Star Date 23:45:06, but people will evidently still believe it.

"I'm a doctor, not an engineer." The human body is more than just machinery, even in the age of technology. Sometimes during a physical exam I do feel like a mechanic, trying to find the tiny rubbing noises and mysterious squeaking sounds of the body before small problems become big ones. It is even easier on the Enterprise, where people are hooked up to diagnostic computers, their heart and lung functions measured on sliding scales and digital readouts. Even so, the two jobs are worlds apart. Unlike engineers, doctors have to fix the problem with the engines still running. I'd like to see Scotty try that.

"I'm not perfect, Jim. I'm only human." This takes on an entirely new meaning in a universe populated by hundreds of other intelligent species. Dr. McCoy was human, and that was sometimes his greatest strength. When they set out on their journey to go "where no one had gone before," they brought the technology to keep them healthy, but they also brought the passion and humanity of medicine in Dr. McCoy. No matter how advanced medical science becomes, we will always need that spark of humanity to make it worthwhile.

Star Trek is, of course, only science fiction. I don't have any glowing flashbulb to tell me what is wrong with my patients, and there is no diagnostic computer in our office—at least, not yet. Most of my patients were not zapped by space aliens but by tiny

Are You a Real Doctor?

microscopic particles called viruses. Some of them are even slowly killing themselves with a variety of twentieth-century poisons. Taking care of them means being a bit of a politician, a carpenter, a mind reader, and even a fortune teller. I need to be all these things, especially the last one: human.

That's one thing that is as important now as it will be for Dr. "Bones" McCoy in the twenty-third century.

Dear Dr. DePaolis:

Some mysterious person dropped a copy of "Where No Doctor Has Gone Before" in my mailbox, and this note is to thank you and the person who made the delivery.

I appreciate your kind comments. It was a lovely article, and I am extremely pleased that I might have had something to do with pointing you toward your chosen career. I am certain you will find fulfillment and success.

To quote a certain Vulcan, "Live long and prosper."

To Dr. DePaolis, the real McCoy,
from DeForest Kelley, the reel McCoy

What's in the Pockets?

Consider the long white coat, the standard uniform of the modern doctor.

Why do doctors wear them? Do they use them to cover their clothing, in case they forgot to wear a belt that day? Or because they only have to iron a small V-shaped section on the front of their shirts? No, those aren't the reasons. Well, not the main reason, anyway.

We wear white coats because they have pockets. I don't think I could see patients without my pockets; I need the things I carry there.

We learn the habit as interns and residents, a time when we are always on the move between patients. Interns carry entire medical libraries around with them, in convenient spiral format, along with flashlights, hammers, pins, and small vials of smelly things to test olfactory nerve function. Later, when we settle down into offices of our own, we still rely on the comfortable feel of full pockets as we do our daily work.

Are You a Real Doctor?

What is in there? What could be so important? To find out, let's take a tour of the pockets in my own white coat that I wear during a day of family practice. While this may become personally revealing, I am willing to offer this insight for a good cause. Medical research is never easy.

The most obvious thing in my pockets is the stethoscope that sticks out on one side. Of course I keep this near me, having lost about thirty of them since I graduated medical school. It is usually draped around my neck or hanging limply out of one pocket. A stethoscope is very useful in examining the rest of the contents of that pocket, because every time I pull it out it dumps everything else out onto the floor. That's why I usually keep it around my neck, and that's why it is usually cold when the time comes to use it.

Here's a pad of blank prescriptions. Over the last few years I have become paranoid about leaving these lying around, so I always carry them with me. Can't do that without large pockets.

Let's see, here are some pens. "Some" is a variable term, ranging from a few to somewhere in the low triple digits. Pens tend to accumulate over time, and the more pens in your pocket, the more chance that one of them will leak ink onto the white coat. That's how you know it is time to get a clean coat. This will continue to happen until doctors feel comfortable with plastic pocket protectors like they wear at the gas station.

Moving across to the other side, it is hard to tell exactly what is in this pocket. All I can see are hundreds of little plastic stickers. We have a basket of these stickers that we keep near our children's exam room, but I keep these with me because these are the "good" ones: Superman, Mickey, Ninja turtles, things like that. I save these for my best patients. So far, every child I have ever seen has been a "best" patient, so I go through a lot of them.

Pushing the stickers aside I can see a bunch of tongue depressors and some small sugar packets. These are used mostly to prepare coffee in the morning. I carry these wooden sticks around like we don't have a big tub full of them in every patient room.

Now we move to the heart of the pocket system, the upper left chest pocket. Riding high over the larger side pockets, held close to the breast, the things in this pocket are the most important of all. This is the information and scheduling center, where dozens of small notes to myself are collected for future reference. Here's one that reminds me to call a patient and see if she is getting better. Here's another telling me to call the washer-dryer repair man. There are notes that prompt me to read the textbook chapter on thyroid disease, buy a new pair of mittens, send in the registration for a conference—these are the vital pieces of information that might otherwise be lost without this important pocket.

Oh, yes, a pair of scissors is also jammed between the slips of paper, a recent addition to my white coat. My days have gone so much smoother since I started keeping a scissors with me. I use it for a hundred things a day. Now I never have to waste precious time digging through drawers when I need to remove a bandage or open a letter. I have several million dollars worth of medical equipment at my disposal every day, from audiometers to MRI scanners, and the thing I appreciate the most is a $2.98 pair of scissors.

The last thing on the coat is my name tag, perched on the edge of the breast pocket. I am proud of my name tag; I feel almost naked without it. I don't think I would feel like a real doctor if it wasn't there, no matter how much stuff is in the other pockets.

No wonder I wear a white coat. I don't know how anyone can get along without one. One of my partners went for several years in just a shirt and tie, but he eventually realized the value of the coat. One day he finally decided to put one on, and he has worn it ever since.

Of course, that was also the day he forgot his belt.

Act Like a Doctor

"But soft! What light in yonder tonsil breaks! 'Tis the strep, and uvula is the sun."

This is the way I've been talking since I read "Acting in Medical Practice," an article that said all doctors should take acting lessons.

The article appeared in the serious British medical journal *The Lancet*. This is one of two main sources for boring medical news, the other being the New England Journal of the American Medical Association (NEJAMA, not to be confused with the Terribly Obscure English Journal for Associated Medical Americans, or TOEJAMA).

Using very long words, the authors urged doctors to take acting classes so they could convey an attitude of caring and concern to their patients. Messages of understanding and support have been shown to help patients and their families, even when faked.

This is an interesting theory which makes a lot of sense if you believe that doctors are selfish, insensitive worms. The article went on to say this kind of emotional support is too important to depend on a doctor's moods. Doctors, they maintain, are under stress (although not as much as patients, who are sick) and many of them

Act Like a Doctor

are too tired or cranky to show genuine concern. If they can't make themselves care, the authors suggest, then they should at least pretend.

This goes along with things parents have been saying for years. "Well, at least take a few acting classes," they often warn their children who apply to medical school. "At least then if the doctor thing doesn't work out you'll have something to fall back on."

While the idea of simulated compassion seems tacky, most medical students are already getting plenty of this kind of teaching, between memorizing effective interviewing techniques, practicing nonverbal communication skills, and watching old reruns of M*A*S*H.

In my medical school we had weekly lessons in acting like doctors, where we would practice wearing white coats and looking concerned. Later we took our act on the road to several local hospitals, where everyone was convinced we were real physicians except for the nurses, ward clerks, lab technicians, physical therapists, maintenance workers, teen-aged candy stripers, and patients.

Luckily, the test was a written exam. Still, doctors have been playing these roles for a long time. For example, in the past, surgeons often played maniacal tyrants who threw sharpened surgical instruments during choreographed outbursts in operating theaters. Now they are more like the doctors on *Chicago Hope,* who stop on their way to deliver medicine to poor asthmatic children in order to perform emergency limb reattachments for charity.

There was never any reason for doctors to take formal acting classes, unless they were going to star in their own late-night TV ads like lawyers do ("Have you ever been infected by a virus or bacterial particle? Dial 1-800-HEALING today. Fee in advance.").

Now, with this new study, drama can become an official part of the medical school curriculum, like golf and ignoring gross bodily fluids. With this training, doctors will be able to use new approaches to difficult medical problems:

Problem: Patient won't take medicine.
Old way: Doctor pleads with them to be compliant.

Are You a Real Doctor?

New way: Doctor stuffs cotton in cheeks, mumbles dramatically while making them "an offer they can't refuse."

Problem: Insomnia.
Old way: Doctor prescribes sleeping pill.
New way: Doctor comes to the home and performs a scene from a Chekhov play or any Merchant Ivory movie featuring Helena Bonham-Carter.

Problem: Obesity.
Old way: Doctor gives a printed diet sheet.
New way: Music swells as doctor stands in front of brilliant sunset, tears welling up, and makes the emotional, heart-rending promise, "As God is my witness, you will always be hungry again."

While this would be entertaining, most doctors are already showing authentic, genuine concern for their patients, being human beings and not sea slugs. Drama lessons would only turn them into intense, brooding method actors. Imagine telling your problems to Robert DeNiro in *Taxi Driver*. ("Are you bleeding on me? ARE YOU BLEEDING ON ME?")

At least this might have fooled the candy stripers.

Nerd Processing—Computers in Medicine

There's good news for people traveling on the information superhighway, especially the ones getting into accidents: medical help is closer than ever as more and more doctors are using computers.

This is not really news. Computers are changing the way everyone does their jobs, and many clinics and doctor's offices are now going digital. Someday visiting your doctor will be every bit as fast and easy as dealing with the IRS.

Until just recently, medicine lagged behind other businesses in this area. This is surprising because most doctors love new technology, being very close to geeks themselves. Most medical offices have used computers only for billing purposes. This allowed accountants to keep each record up to date, making sure that every patient quickly and efficiently received the wrong bill.

Are You a Real Doctor?

The other main medical use of computers has been in high-tech diagnostic tests like CAT scans, which use precise beams of X-rays to discover whether your body contains any household pets. Newer computerized scans have become so incredibly sensitive that they can even detect thoughts as they form in the brain, the most common thought being "I can't wait until this scan is over."

Now this is all changing. One reason is the invention of the CD-ROM, a small silver disc that can hold an incredible amount of computerized data or the sound track from *Wayne's World 2*. Imagine a CD-ROM disc that could contain the entire text of every book ever written by Stephen King. They can't, of course—all the CD-ROMs currently in existence couldn't—but still, they can hold a lot.

Like textbooks. This is important to doctors because they are always looking up things like the names of the various wrist bones or the correct dose of the antidepressant featured that morning on *Sally Jesse Raphael*. Most of them have large shelves in their offices lined with heavy medical textbooks, which they use for research and as backdrops when TV news reporters interview them about startling, late-breaking medical news like the fact that chocolate is addictive.

Now they need only a few CDs on the shelf instead. This makes all that information instantly accessible by computer and frees up valuable space for their videotapes of *ER*.

Naturally, this will affect the way medical students are taught. One major medical school recently provided all incoming students with powerful laptop computers containing the entire medical school curriculum. The students, sensing they were on the verge of a new era in medical training, promptly gave them back.

Most medical students like textbooks. They are proud of the fact that they can't even lift what they have to know. For them, a computer is a poor substitute for a book, especially when they fall asleep on their notes at 3:00 A.M. with their faces in puddles of drool. They prefer old-fashioned methods, like boring lectures and dirty mnemonics.

Despite the whining, computers are already changing the way doctors learn. Specialty board exams now use computerized

Nerd Processing—Computers in Medicine

medical simulations, presenting complex medical cases and even scenes from actual surgery. This makes them like video games, only with less blood. "Game over" has an entirely new meaning in these simulations.

Some education programs even use multimedia to recreate the sights and sounds of actual patient visits, which doctors do all day long. This is like Neil Armstrong playing Lunar Lander. Doctors would be better off playing useful games like Star Wars Rebel Assault, which can help them use "the force" (medical knowledge) to fight for the oppressed (indigent) against the forces of evil (insurance companies) who serve the dark lord (Newt Gingrich.)

Even more importantly, computers have become useful in actual medical situations, where they can help doctors take better care of patients. There are programs that can consider a list of symptoms and come up with the most likely diagnosis for that patient. Some of them can even decide on the proper treatment, coming up with a specific medication.

All this points to the day when doctor's offices will be entirely computerized, like on-line banking services. Medicine will finally leap forward into the twenty-first century, where computers will be an integral part of every doctor visit as they automatically answer the phone, make the appointment, record the symptoms, scan the entire body, make the diagnosis, select the treatment, print the prescription, and send the wrong bill.

Dr. Superman

Look! Up in the sky! It's a bird! It's a plane! It's—a primary care provider?

It is now. This month in the latest issue of *Superman,* the man of steel actually delivers a baby.

I was just as surprised as all the other physicians who were reading through their new comics and saw Superman performing this kind of doctor work. It hardly seems fair. I mean, I hardly ever get to rescue people from burning airplanes or flooding rivers.

Still, I have to put aside my petty jealousy and focus on the real question: As a doctor, how did he do?

To find out, I gave him a call. Well, not directly. It's hard to talk to Superman himself because, as most people know, he is unlisted. Besides, Metropolis is a long way from anywhere, being a fictional city like Hope, Arkansas.

Instead, I did the next best thing. Dan Jurgens, the writer and artist for *Superman,* happens to live in a split-level Fortress of Solitude here in the suburbs of Minneapolis. I called him instead and asked him to speak for the Man of Steel:

Dr. Superman

Q: Superman, how did you happen to deliver a baby?

A: It was during a snowstorm. The power was out when the police got a call from a woman who lived on the fifty-third floor of a building. I was going to fly her to the hospital, but it was too late to move her, so I helped her deliver there.

Q: You seemed a little nervous—why? It wasn't as bad as fighting super villains, was it?

A: Well, I've never done it before. Plus, babies are so small. I'm used to handling much bigger things, like evil robots or runaway trains. For a guy like me, who can bend steel in his mighty hands, it was a little scary.

Q: You used your X-ray vision to see the baby. Was this a problem?

A: No, my X-ray vision works differently than regular X-ray machines. It was completely safe. I only mentioned it to the mother because I didn't want her to worry.

Q: Were your other superpowers helpful?

A: Oh, yes, certainly. Boiling water, for example, was a snap.

Q: Did your patient say anything during delivery?

A: Yes, she said, and I'm quoting here, "AAAOWWW!" I didn't need super hearing for that one.

Q: I noticed you used your cape during the delivery, then you put it back on and flew away.

A: Yes, I used it to wrap the baby.

Q: I wonder if that was really a good idea. I've done a lot of deliveries myself, and they get pretty, well, messy.

A: You're telling me. Like Lois said, I really should have flown through a car wash on my way home. I ended up using my heat vision on it later.

Q: It sounds like things went very well. In fact, someone at the hospital said you would make a good surgeon. Did you ever think about being a doctor?

A: I don't think I would have the skill, the dedication, or the endurance for it. After all, I'm only Superman. Plus, my malpractice insurance is a lot lower.

Are You a Real Doctor?

Once again, Superman saved the day. He performed a delivery as well as any doctor could have done. Maybe even better, considering the way he handled the mess.

Afterward he changed into his secret identity, newspaper columnist Clark Kent, and went off to do an interview that he used to write a column much better than this one.

That's OK—I'm getting used to it.

Dental Plan

Every trained medical person knows the value of regular checkups, which is why I have always made it a point to visit my dentist every ten years whether I need to or not.

I know—this is like telling a doctor, "Why should I have a physical? I haven't had any heart attacks yet." For me it's even dumber because my dentist is a friend of mine. If I had to show my teeth to a stranger I would probably wait until I could send them via overnight express delivery.

Naturally, I feel guilty about this, and so I floss. A lot. I can do this thanks to my Floss-O-Matic, a wonderful hand-held flossing device. It is simple, it is convenient, and it is a neon red color that is visible even from the bathroom next door, making it impossible to ignore even when sleepy.

Insufficient flossing is the reason most people don't like to go to the dentist. They know dentists always ask them how often they floss, just like they know they will surely lie. You can't tell a dentist that you have been flossing like clockwork every Olympic year, if you count picking your teeth with those little cards that fall out of magazines. "Oh, several times a week," you say instead, jumping sideways to avoid any lightning bolts. While I hadn't been to a dentist since Ronald Reagan's first term, I was sure my flosser had kept my teeth in shape, saving me from dental ridicule.

Now it was here again, a year with a 5 in it, and walking into the dentist's office I immediately recognized one thing: the smell. Nothing else smells like a dentist's office, a not-unpleasant mixture of disinfectant and mint, with just a hint of mind-numbing anesthetic gas. I sat under a colorful chart showing proper brushing technique and filled out the patient form. There, after name, address, and toothpaste brand, was the section on flossing, with questions like this:

Q: How many times a week do you floss?

Q: No, Really.

Q: OK, if that's your story.

There were other questions about pneumonia, heart disease, and diabetes, but as far as I know my teeth never had any of those things. Another asked, "Would you change the appearance of your teeth if you could?" I later learned this is because modern dentistry has come a long way in improving the way teeth look, including letting people select a new tooth color. I chose "43: Stark Winter Ivory." Next month I'm having cheek implants.

My dentist then asked me whether I wanted him to take a full series of dental X-rays. As a doctor, I try to avoid X-raying body parts that seem healthy. Dentists do X-rays to pick up early signs of cavities and because they don't like to get sued. We settled on a plan where he agreed not to take any unneeded X-rays and I promised to have cavities only in obvious, easy-to-reach locations. There were no witnesses to corroborate this.

Instead, he took a series of video pictures of my teeth, which he showed to me on a small monitor labeled ORAL-VISION. This gave me a chance to see what my saliva would look like if some TV network executive gave it a sitcom. He printed copies, I assume for the "dental records" you hear about in newscasts and disaster movies. Clearly, the message was, "Go ahead and have that fiery car wreck. We're ready."

He then began the exam. My dentist is an interesting guy, and I always look forward to seeing him socially. Working in different health fields, we often have stimulating discussions about the philosophy and economics of medicine, including the effects of health reform on the future of America. This time things were a little different, in that I couldn't talk at all and he spent the time poking me with metal hooks.

While he worked I was focused on one thought: where am I supposed to put my tongue? With a full-grown dentist in my mouth, my tongue suddenly had no place to rest. It writhed and twisted like a python on a triple espresso. This didn't seem to bother my dentist. In fact, at one point he even checked under my tongue and said, "looks good." I took this as a compliment, figuring the underside of my tongue could play a supporting role in the "Saliva" show, possibly as the wacky neighbor.

Unfortunately, although I use my Floss-O-Matic daily, I learned that I haven't been flossing correctly. No gadget can replace good dental hygiene, which was never meant to be convenient. Proper flossing, as demonstrated by my dentist, involves (1) pain, and (2) bleeding, and neither was covered in the flosser instruction booklet.

Otherwise, things went pretty well. I had one cavity, and there is a little problem with my wisdom teeth (they grew in sideways—how wise is that?), but on the whole, visiting my dentist was pleasant, informative, and relatively painless, and I'm not just saying that because he will soon be working close to my face with power tools.

I even promised to go back in six months, much sooner than my usual schedule. I left with a new toothbrush and a warm, inner glow that comes from doing the right thing. Or maybe it was the gas.

Fitting into Your Fat Genes

There has been a lot of exciting news recently about fat. You might think the fat question was figured out years ago—you eat the food, you become the food—but a recent batch of plump, juicy stories about obesity proves that scientists are still working on it. This lets them avoid the really hard medical questions, like why hospital gowns that tie in four places still won't stay closed in the back.

In one recent breakthrough, scientists announced that they had found the gene that produces obesity. It was located on William Shatner.

No, actually, the gene was discovered in mice. Scientists believe that the gene produces proteins that trigger the feeling of fullness, the signal to stop eating. In some mice, however, this gene is mutated and defective, providing no feedback and turning them into furry little Hostess Sno Balls with ears.

A lot of people were happy about this discovery. They believe this research finally figured out the real reason they are overweight, as if all those Dove Bars count for nothing.

Fitting into Your Fat Genes

While the gene theory is attractive, it's probably not the reason that Americans have been getting fatter over the last thirty years. For one thing, anything even remotely connected with genetics takes forever. Even a single medical school lecture on genetics takes years to end. The increase in American waistlines happened much too rapidly to be a product of mutated genes, following instead the rise of cable TV stations and Taco Bells.

Besides, even if bad genes are the reason, this is no help for losing weight. So far, scientists only know where the gene is, not how to fix it. (Everyone knows where Bosnia is, too.) If anything, this discovery means that people will have to be even more careful to stay away from things like chocolate and tortilla chips, knowing their chromosomes could overpower them at any moment.

Maybe that's why former Surgeon General C. Everett Koop chose that same week to announce his new crusade against obesity, called "Shape Up America!" Koop appeared at a big health reform pep rally with Hillary Rodham Clinton, saying that one out of three Americans are overweight. The president himself did not appear with them, which would have proved his point.

"Eat sensibly. Exercise. Drop a few pounds. Shape up," advised the seventy-eight-year-old pediatric surgeon, who was promoting his new exercise video, *Sweating with Epaulets*.

Notice he never said, "and sign up at your neighborhood weight loss clinic." That's because on that very same day a panel of fat scientists—that is, scientists who study fat—released a report calling these clinics a waste of money, in a industry that makes billions of dollars off of people who never lose any weight. In fact, the scientists could find no real evidence that these places do any good at all, just hundreds of grainy before-and-after photos showing different people holding up what appear to be the same pair of enormous pants.

Most of these clinics ask you to follow a very specific diet plan, their plan, requiring you to buy and eat their food, from their kitchens, off their dishes, while sitting in their living rooms in front of their TVs afterward. No wonder people never lose weight—the plans are boring, and everyone knows the number one treatment for boredom is snack therapy.

Are You a Real Doctor?

The panel urged people to see a doctor before joining any of these plans, mainly so the doctor can talk them out of it. Doctors can help people focus on the right approach. If not, they can at least give them a variety of non-boring diet plans to pick from.

Take a look at these actual diets from an average hospital menu:

- The wired jaw diet

- The minimum residue, low fiber, limited dairy products diet

- The T & A diet (Sorry—that's for tonsils and adenoids.)

- The six feedings a day, balanced small meals and snacks diet

- The anti-infection diet, limiting food containing germs and bacteria

- The high-calorie diet

This, not stories about bad genes or weight loss scams, is the kind of useful information that can really make a difference. Many of you may be already following one of these diets. Six feedings per day is considered standard at our house, seven on holidays.

If you're not, maybe you should, and here I am thinking specifically of people eating a lot of germs and bacteria. Remember—eat the food, become the food. It's only genetic.

The TV News Doctor Audition

I have never been very impressed with the doctors on television news shows. Most of them supposedly report on health and medical news, and their hard-hitting, insightful reports have always managed to get me thinking. What I'm usually thinking is: "That job doesn't look so hard. I could do that."

What an easy thing to say while sitting on the couch at home. Now I know it is not as easy as it looks. When the lights go on and the camera is pointed at your own flushed and sweaty face, things seem very different.

Last summer one of our local stations needed a new medi-cal reporter. They ran an ad in the state medical journal, and one of my friends pointed it out to me. I'm not sure why. I have never wanted to be on TV. Well, of course I have, but never enough to consider a career change. I like my practice, and I had no intention of giving it up for show business.

Still, it was an interesting idea. It would be fun to prove that I had what it takes, I told myself. It would be an adventure. I made a few calls and sent in a résumé. A week later, I learned I had landed myself an audition for the role of "news doctor."

I was excited about the audition, and I decided to do a little research for the role. I watched medical reporters on other channels. Most of their stories had the same general theme: "Things that can secretly kill you." There was a shocking story about radon gas that could leak into your basement and secretly kill you, a hard-hitting exposé on side effects of prescription drugs that could kill you, and an alarming piece on chemical food additives that could make you sick, if not kill you. On the lighter side, there was also a disturbing look at junk mail that could give you bad paper cuts.

I learned that most TV news shows present a very sensational view of medicine. Rather than provide good advice they focus on the most lurid and shocking aspects of life—just like everything else on TV.

My careful research also revealed another important consideration: I was not good-looking enough for TV news. These guys had obviously used their modeling fees to pay for medical school. As you can see from the photo on the cover, I was forced to rely on student loans instead.

Together, these two important facts made me realize that I was not really news doctor material, but I decided to go ahead with the audition anyway. I thought it would be fun, and if nothing else I would have a souvenir, a tape of myself on the news. I could always show it at parties, or keep it in my dresser drawer forever, depending on my performance.

I arrived at the studio a few minutes early. As I waited my turn, I looked at the information sheet they had given me to fill out. Some of the questions were peculiar. Along with a list of schools and background information they also asked for my shirt and shoe sizes. Hair color, eye color, body build, hat size—this form was certainly different from the one that got me into medical school. Besides, I had no idea what my hat size is. I use the third hole in the plastic strap of my Minnesota Twins cap, but there was no room to write that on the form.

I was feeling nervous but confident as I waited my turn. Finally the door opened, and the previous applicant stepped out of the studio.

My confidence disappeared. This woman looked like she had just run ten miles. Her neat, tailored suit was severely wrinkled, her string tie hanging limply from one collar button, and her blouse was covered with large damp spots. Evidently TV news was more demanding than I realized, but there was nothing I could do because it was now my turn.

I walked into the studio. The glare of the lights made it hard to see the director, but he welcomed me and showed me to my spot behind a large desk. He told me where to look and what to watch for during the audition. He wished me luck. In a few seconds, he gave me my cue, the red light on the camera started to flash, and I was "on."

We had been asked to prepare a short speech to read on-camera. After all the sensationalism I wanted to present a different view of medicine. I talked about physical exams—who needs one, how often you should go, and what kind of tests are important. It was a talk about staying healthy, not getting killed.

I thought I did fairly well. I had practiced enough to make my delivery smooth, and I knew where my important points were. My high school speech teacher would have been proud. I put my heart into it, and was satisfied that I had done my best.

Then the director gave me a tolerant smile and said, "All right. Fine. Very good—for a run-through. Now, let's do it for real, and this time look at the camera."

During the next thirty minutes I must have read my speech a half a dozen times. By the last time, I had no idea what I was saying anymore. At that point, the director joined me on stage, and in a jocular voice he asked me several questions about general physicals. It was a test to see if I could perform the quick, happy banter that most TV news teams use between stories. It is hard to be clever in front of a camera.

By the end I was tired and sweating, and I felt like I had run ten miles. I left the studio, went home and put on my Twins cap.

What happened after the audition? Nothing. It's been six years, and I'm still waiting to hear from them. I suspect the station didn't like my approach to TV news. Either that, or they felt funny hiring someone with a hat size of 3.

The station now has a new medical reporter. They may just be using him until they make up their mind, although he is pretty good-looking. I saw him the other night, doing a story on houseplants that could secretly kill you. Now that I know what it is like in front of the camera, I have to admit that he was pretty good.

Paging the Rug Doctor

I rarely use the title "doctor" when I am away from my office. At work it sounds natural, but at other times, in other places, it still sounds weird to me. I often stumble when I call myself "doctor" in public, just like I did when I was a medical student.

Other people use the title "doctor" all the time. It is no wonder people get confused about all the different medical specialties. There are all kinds of doctors around, and not all of them are physicians. Who are all these people?

Some of them also work in the health care field. I have often wondered if these other professionals would rather have their own, more descriptive titles. Maybe a dentist would rather be called "dentor," eliminating any confusion from the start. Veterinarians might prefer "vettor," or even better, "dogtor."

Even so, that would still leave a lot of "doctors." I took a look through our local phone book, and I was surprised by how often the word "doctor" appeared.

Most of the listings were in the residential section, where people

Are You a Real Doctor?

named Doctor filled one whole column. Most of them used a slightly different spelling—there is probably some federal regulation covering this—but it can still be confusing. The most common spelling was Dockter, with several Docters and one Docktor. Obviously, this kind of thing is bound to happen, and these people should not be blamed. Most of them had nothing to say about the spelling of their names.

I moved on to the yellow pages. There were pages of physician listings, including one Doctor Dockter, or Doctor 2 (doctor squared.) At first glance this seems excessive, but it was really a special case. This person probably went to medical school just to put a stop to the teasing that began in junior high school. Clearly, he or she had the last laugh.

I looked for a few more minutes before I realized that I was coming dangerously close to doing actual research, something I normally try to avoid. Regardless, I decided to press on. I turned to the business section, where my investigation revealed several suspicious listings.

There was the "Bike Doctor," evidently someone who practiced the healing arts on spokes and handlebars.

"The Pet Doktor" was also listed. This was not, as you would suspect, a veterinarian's office but a pet store. The owner just happened to be named Doktor, they told me when I called.

There was a listing for a computer repair person named "The Disk Doctor." The number was disconnected.

There were no lawyers named Doctor.

There were no "Auto Doctors," although I did find a Muffler Clinic, where there were several "exhaust system specialists" ready to perform a consultation on my car.

I was becoming even more skeptical. How can one word be used to describe so many different jobs? Did the title "Doctor" mean nothing anymore?

I turned the page, and a name caught my eye. There, listed under "Carpet & Rug Cleaning, (Cont'd)," was a small, tasteful ad for "The Rug Doctor."

Who was this Rug Doctor, I wondered? Was it a real doctor?

Someone who became fed up with medicine, abandoning his or her practice and escaping into a world of steam cleaners and Scotchguard? I decided to find out. Picking up the phone, I dialed the number.

The phone rang three times before a recorded message came on. "I am unable to personally answer your call," said the voice.

Already, I was noticing significant differences between this practice and my own. I could never use an answering machine to take calls.

I called again later, and this time my call was answered personally. I heard the same voice say, "Rug doctor, can I help you?"

"Can I please speak to the doctor?" I asked.

The man hesitated for a moment. "This is the rug doctor," he said finally. I expected something like this. Everyone always says it is not easy to get a doctor on the phone.

After all this investigating I was starting to feel like Mike Wallace. Pretending to be just a routine customer, I casually asked about the business.

"We rent carpet cleaners," he said simply. "We're a franchise for rental equipment."

"You don't even do the work yourself?"

"Nope. Just rent."

I was shocked. What kind of doctor was this? I could never call myself a doctor if all I did was rent people the instruments and textbooks to diagnose their own illnesses. "And Rug Doctor—is he or she a real doctor?"

The man laughed. "No, that's just the name. It was started by the original owners. They just liked the way it sounded."

My suspicions were true: there was no doctor at The Rug Doctor. I wanted to ask a few more questions, but by now the man had figured out that I did not want to rent a carpet cleaner. He said good-bye and hung up.

As I had suspected, the word "doctor" is no guarantee. A lot of people use the title, whether they have earned it or not. I guess a title means nothing in itself; it is only as good as the person behind it.

Are You a Real Doctor?

On the other hand, there is no reason for me to feel awkward about using the word in public. I have as much right to call myself a "doctor" as the bike, the pet, or the rug doctors do. After all, if Mike Wallace ever calls to check up on me, I won't have a thing to hide.

Medical Christmas Shopping

Each year in early December people start worrying if they don't have all their presents wrapped and under the tree. With the crowds and the weather making it impossible to get to stores, many of them get desperate for last-minute shopping time.

Luckily, the first part of winter is also the cold and flu season. While it may be hard for people to get to a store, many of them will be going to the doctor. Most people don't realize how many beautiful and practical gifts can be found at the average medical office. Here are some suggestions:

Aspirin ($1.89, various makers)

Aspirin, one of the first medicines, is still one of the most useful. It helps headaches and muscle strains, dissolves blood clots, and even prevents heart attacks and strokes. Many people take an aspirin every day. It can be a thoughtful and economical gift, especially since aspirin is one product that costs the same no matter how much you buy. Any size bottle, whether a small vial of fifty or a giant economy vat of five hundred costs $1.89. The limiting factor is probably how much wrapping paper you have. This is even true at the airport, where two aspirin tablets and a small paper cup cost $1.89.

Elastic braces ($5–$25, depending on limb)

Every doctor's office carries a variety of braces for minor injuries and simple joint problems. You can get braces for elbows, knees, wrists, ankles, and even little cushioned sleeves for toes. Besides being fashionable, they are easy to mail to your relatives, letting you share the warm holiday sentiment, "Merry Christmas in case you get a sprain."

Flu shot (around $11, major pharmaceutical companies)

As I mentioned, the cold and flu season always comes around Christmas. Give a flu shot to each person on your list, and you will keep them healthy while building strong family traditions for years to come.

Rubber gloves ($4.95, Playtex)

A lot of people want rubber gloves. I know because they ask for them during doctor visits. I suppose they use them for cleaning and other messy jobs around the house, although it is possible—and almost too horrible to consider—that they use them for the same things doctors do. Give a box of 100, and don't ask any questions.

Exercise (free, anywhere)

Everyone needs exercise. Doctors are always telling their patients to get more, but most people just can't find the time, especially during the busy holiday season. This year get some for a loved one, letting him or her avoid the sweat and hassle of staying in shape and living longer. Believe me, you'll both feel better.

Thigh Master ($19.95, stores, mail order, back pages of women's magazines, late-night TV)

No one expects to find these at a medical facility, but when used correctly they can be quite beneficial. We have several in our office, and in clinical testing we have found them to be capable of flinging heavy medical books through the air for a distance of over fifteen feet. We then walk over and pick up the books, exercising those important thigh and back muscles. There is a lot of medical stuff that seems silly and ridiculous at first, but can later turn out to be every bit as useful as a Thigh Master, like the Abdominizer, the Gut Buster, and the doctors on local TV news.

Mole removal (sixty to several hundred dollars, dermatologist)

This is the perfect gift for anyone, as long as they have an ugly mole. Many people can't afford to have these removed, forcing them to wear turtlenecks even in summer. Now, with a gift of pre-paid minor surgery, they can finally go swimming again, although not until the stitches come out.

Cough and cold medicines ($1.59–$4.39, depending on coupons)

As everyone knows, it is the cold and flu. . . . Sooner or later everyone will need some nonprescription cough syrup. While there are roughly 3,000 over-the-counter cough and cold products, they all contain the same five ingredients in varying combinations. Your best bet would be one of the all-purpose, cold-cough-allergy-body aches-congestion-fever medicines, preferably grape, in a forty-eight-ounce holiday gift bucket with convenient carrying handle. Make sure to wait until the other gifts are opened, since anyone who takes it will wake up sometime around New Year's Eve.

Gift certificate ($1 to $1 million, depending on insurance coverage)

Can't make up your mind? Tell that special person you are thinking about them with a gift certificate for medical care. This could let them have that major operation they have been putting off since their insurance company dropped them for having a sore throat. Or maybe a general checkup, giving them a better chance to stick around for a while. They'll never forget you were the one who finally got them to a doctor, who then spent the entire time telling them to lose those extra holiday pounds.

So make it a medical Christmas. Thoughtful presents like these that allow you to give the gift of good health, while sparing you a difficult, or even hazardous, trip to the store.

And, more importantly, gifts like these let me finish my own personal shopping each year without even leaving work.

Dr. Mark's Fun-Time Clinic

People always ask me if I always wanted to be a doctor. The answer, despite what I wrote on my medical school application, is no. I wanted to be a TV kiddie show host.

There were a lot of these shows when I was growing up, like Captain Ken's Steamboat, Clancy the Cop, Axel's Treehouse, and Casey Jones. Even kids that required low-grade explosives to get out of bed on a school day would voluntarily get up at 6:00 A.M. Saturday mornings to watch cartoons with Sigfreid the Spaceman.

Most people remember shows like these from their own childhood. Some of them in other states were a bit peculiar, judging by friends who remember shows like *Uncle Louie's Garment Office,* with characters like second cousin Burton who lived in the shed.

I wanted my own kiddie show. If they had ever called, I would have been ready. I used to stage regular rehearsals in my bedroom. I would sing songs, introduce guest stuffed animals, announce birthdays, and describe my lunch attractively displayed on a paper plate.

Are You a Real Doctor?

They never called. I went to medical school instead, but that doesn't mean it is too late:

"Hey, kids, what time is it? Its time again for—DOCTOR MARK'S HEALTH AND FUN-TIME CLINIC." (Show opens on a stage made up as a doctor's office, with medical equipment and exam tables next to a bleacher full of anxious, laughing children.)

"And here he is—Dr. Mark!" (Applause, theme music. Dr. Mark trips onto the stage wearing a tie, long white coat, and colorful Bermuda shorts, along with a head mirror. The effect is like Rex Morgan on laughing gas while sleep-deprived at the beach.

"Ha, ha, boys and girls. Welcome to Fun-Time Clinic. Please have your insurance information ready. Today we'll learn about avoiding pesky respiratory infections and flossing, along with a visit from Robbie the retro-virus.

"But first, let's see what's in the grab bag for today. OK, there's some Band-Aids . . . hepatitis vaccine . . . syrup of ipecac, good for inducing vomiting . . . and from the hospital cafeteria, cheese sandwiches, also good for vomiting.

"Hey, wait a minute—look over there!" (Actor in feline costume prances on stage with a spotlight, shining it around the set.) "It's Tabby the Cat Scanner. What is it, Tabby? Is something wrong?" (Light falls on small actor in a gray costume huddled under the exam table, who gets up and scampers around the stage.) "Hey, it's Chester Cholesterol! Get out of here! Kids, what do we say?" (Kids scream, "Fat free! Fat free!" Actors run off.) "OK, it's time for our first cartoon."

(Cartoon begins, showing despicable cat chasing lovable mouse into a kitchen, where the mouse hits him in the head with a frying pan. Cat is then transported via airlift helicopter to regional trauma center, where he undergoes emergency craniotomy for subdural hemorrhage followed by several days of intensive care in the neuro recovery unit. Mouse is arraigned on felony assault charges and sentenced to community service, besides a civil judgment of $1.6 million. The message, clearly, is: Don't try this at home.)

"Wasn't that great? Now it's time for Dr. Mark's Corner." (Children form around him in a circle on the floor.) "You know, kids, there are a lot of things I learned in medical school that I wish I knew back when I was your age.

"Like, kids, you know what? You won't really put your eye out. Mom is just saying that so you won't shoot Nerf rockets in the house. Next time, tell her, 'Oh, Mom, scleral tissue is much too resilient. Without some sort of sharpened metal edge, frankly, I just don't see it happening.'

"And no matter what your teacher says, your eyes won't really 'stay that way,' either. Go ahead and cross them when she's not looking. And that 'going blind' thing? Forget about it.

"OK, we'll go back to cartoons after these messages and a quick look at your ears, so don't go away."

All right, maybe it is too late. Even with such positive messages, a show like this would never work today. There's no market for this stuff anymore. Captain Ken was retired into Grandpa Ken, and later disappeared altogether. Casey Jones does oldies radio at a retirement resort up north. Clancy the Cop was demoted to public affairs shows on Sunday mornings before being relegated to voice-overs for jewelry commercials.

Between organized sports, classes, and activities, kids are just too busy to hang out in TV clubhouses anymore. They don't get up early unless they have to, especially when they are exhausted from 3:00 A.M. hockey practice. Instead they have *Power Rangers,* which requires no conscious thought to watch (or produce.)

Just in case, though, I'll keep rehearsing while doing my regular job of being a doctor. "Hey, kids, what time is it? It's INOCULATION TIME! Nurse Deb, what do we have for the patient?"

You see? Except for the Bermuda shorts, it's not all that different.

Infection Reflection

I'm glad I'm a doctor, because medicine can be a very reassuring field, except for the times when it scares you out of your mind.

This is reflected in the recent trend toward terrifying medical entertainment. It began with the recent number one best-selling book, *The Hot Zone*. This is not a story about Sharon Stone, but a largely true account of a dangerous virus that could break loose at any moment and threaten to end civilization as we know it.

Then there was the exciting movie *Outbreak*, which tells the story of a dangerous microbe that breaks loose and threatens to end Dustin Hoffman as we know him. One of the characters is a microbiologist who, like many research scientists, just happens to look like a top fashion supermodel, played by Renee Russo. In the movie's most unbelievable plot twist, she was once married to Hoffman, who looks more like someone who enjoys spending time with infectious microorganisms.

As a kid I used to watch scary movies that featured lumbering giants built from spare parts and man-sized fish creatures with fake

Infection Reflection

rubber gills. I could enjoy these movies because I knew there was statistically very little chance that I would ever run into monsters like these in real life. This allowed me to stay up late watching their movies and, after checking under the bed 2,351 times, still get a full twenty minutes of sleep before school.

Now the more traditional monsters have been replaced by microscopic particles, which are much more scary. I don't want to alarm anyone, but we live in a world teeming with these invisible terrorist intruders that are capable of doing us much more harm than any evil zombie. They surround us at all times and, like politicians, they have the power to destroy us without even realizing it.

Every so often these aggressive infections raise their ugly faces, just to let doctors know who is really in charge. Recently a deadly outbreak of meningitis left most of the Midwest alarmed and confused. We are once again hearing about sporadic cases of invasive killer strep, the so-called flesh-eating bacteria, a comical name for a horrifying disease.

One major university held a seminar on emerging infections. Experts spoke about spooky things like HIV, hepatitis, Streptococcus, meningitis, food poisoning, and tick-borne infections like Lyme disease. The lesson is that bad things can happen to anyone who foolishly risks having unprotected sex, going outdoors, eating, or breathing.

Unfortunately, the fee does not cover the cost of group therapy afterward. I would lock myself in the basement for months, afraid even to talk on the phone for fear of catching something through my long-distance carrier.

Meningitis and strep infections have been around for a long time, but when they surface nowadays they seem even more threatening. We assume medicine has come up with better treatment by now. While new, more expensive antibiotics show up every week, often with strong-sounding names like Fortaz or Suprax, the treatment for infections like strep is still the same—penicillin and lots of it, given early and often until the infection resolves.

Until just recently, that is. In case anyone is still sleeping nights, there are now reports of growing resistance to antibiotics. Some infections are getting stronger; soon they may laugh at plain old penicillin. Doctors will be like criminals trying to kill Superman, watching their powerful antibiotics bounce harmlessly off the new, improved germs, then throwing the empty bottle at them in frustration.

Besides, even the best antibiotics only work on bacteria like strep. Viruses are a whole lot scarier. Doctors have never even pretended to know how to handle viruses. Doctors say, "It's a virus," when they really mean, "Beats me. Let's hope it goes away."

When it doesn't, then things get really creepy. Viruses take your own cells, which are supposed to be busy making more you, and turn them into tiny worker drones that start producing more virus instead. It's like *Invasion of the Body Snatchers,* only without pods.

As you can see, real life is scary enough. We don't need any more books or movies about this particular aspect of medicine. Personally, I'll be happy to stick with something less fearful, like the other recent number one medical best-seller, *How We Die.*

I'll be curled up reading in the basement. Don't bother calling—I know better than to answer the phone.

Dr. Mom

Here is how you can tell if your doctor has kids:

Sometime during a well-child appointment, the doctor may hand you a small rubber ball with a long pointed nozzle and tell you to use this to suck mucus from your baby's nose.

If they say this with a straight face, they do not have any children.

I used to say this all the time, and I really believed it was a good suggestion. Now I have a baby of my own, and I know that any child over the age of three days would never put up with this. Even newborns quickly learn to twist their heads to the side at the first sight of a bulb syringe, and few of them would ever let you perform this kind of thing twice.

This is just one example of the way doctors are woefully unprepared for bringing up children. Despite years of medical school and residency, somehow the important things got missed. It is not until you have a child that you even begin to understand how much you need to know, but were never taught.

In four years of family practice I must have performed hundreds of well-child exams, but I don't think I ever once told a new parent how to mix formula, or how to keep legs still while changing diapers, or how to select a toy that will last longer than forty-eight hours in the hands of an active baby. Granted, some of these nobody knows how to do, like diaper changing, but I still wonder how much good I was doing.

Suddenly, our new son arrived. I immediately reviewed my medical school notes and textbooks looking for advice on how to care for him.

The only medical school subject even remotely related was embryology. The only thing it taught us was that our precious baby had once had gills. This was no help.

Years later, during internship and residency, I spent a lot of time on the pediatrics wards of several busy hospitals. I learned about pediatric neurology, neonatal intensive care, and childhood infectious diseases. I took care of a lot of sick children, but when they got better they went home. Nobody showed me what to do after that.

The class I really needed was never offered. Somewhere in my training I should have spent six weeks in a daycare center, learning basic parenting, a sort of Mother 101 course.

Because of this deficiency, we had to do what all first-time parents do about child care, which is make it up as we go along.

My wife and I share a practice, and we take turns staying home to care for our son. We are in the same specialty, we both went to the same medical school, and we couldn't be more different in the way we spend our days at home.

The two of them play together at home; my son and I go on long walks with him riding my back. We eat when we're hungry; they follow something called a "schedule."

It even shows in the way we dress him. On my wife's day off, our son is dressed in cute matching outfits, as many as four or five a day, judging from the pile of laundry that builds up. In fact, he dresses a lot like she does. They both look very nice.

On my days, he wears his jeans and an old sweatshirt, kind of like—well, you get the idea.

Our son doesn't seem to mind. "He likes the variety," we tell people. "He is learning to be flexible." If that's true, we have stumbled onto a valuable parenting technique entirely by accident.

Of course, we have learned a lot since we became parents. My wife reads a lot of parenting books, but I have been learning from the same source my own mother used: other mothers.

I used to give lectures during well-child exams. Now I listen as much as I talk. I tell the parents about immunizations and developmental milestones, and in return I learn some different tricks for getting kids into bed, or a new way to get them to eat things they hate. I can then pass these tips on to other parents who bring their children in. I have become a kind of clearinghouse for parent-child advice. I go past the allotted appointment time by five or ten minutes because I stay in the room so long, and I know the experience has become a lot more valuable for everyone.

Once in a while I even bring out the rubber bulb syringe, but now I do it mostly to relax jittery new parents. "When the baby gets congested, just use this to suck out the mucus," I tell them, and then we both have a good laugh. "Seriously," I say finally, "you might as well just follow them around with a tissue. I know it's a bother, but it's better than having to wrestle them to the ground."

The parents nod, knowing that I understand what they're going through. They leave thinking that I must have gone to a great medical school.

Life Lessons on the Ant Farm

There is no better way to teach children about working together in a happy, productive community than getting an ant farm. At least, I sure hope this is true, because I wouldn't want to go through it for nothing.

Yes, they still make ant farms. My sister gave one to our son for his birthday, an obvious attempt to pay us back for the "rhythm set" we gave her kids the year before, a collection of percussion toys that made more noise than a fraternity party on an airport runway.

Still, despite any hidden meaning, my son enjoyed his ant farm and played with it happily for months. Then my sister ruined everything by asking him when he would be getting some ants.

The farm came with no ants, but with a card to send away for them. Things were going so well I ignored it, but she insisted. "C'mon, they're the perfect pets," she said. "You only have to feed them once a week, and if you forget, they eat each other." I had to admit, this seemed like an important life lesson. I mailed the card and $1.75 to Indiana, where ants evidently come from.

Life Lessons on the Ant Farm

The ants arrived 4 to 6 weeks later. We were worried that they would not survive a postal trip during cold weather, but the first instruction on the box told us to put it in the freezer. This slows down the ants and makes them easier to catch when they try to escape, and they do.

The box held a complete set of ants, all male, along with another card to send away for more ants, also male. "Don't try this at home," was the obvious message from the people manufacturing ants. Including this second card was a clever marketing ploy and an omen for our future as ant farmers.

After 30 minutes the ants were properly sluggish, and we only lost a few when we dumped them through the opening slot onto the fresh sand of their new farm home.

It is strange to see ants in your kitchen and not give in to your first instinct, which is to stomp on them. We were, in fact, feeding them, giving them daily allotments of sugar water and little slivers of food.

These were not for eating, but for transporting. Carrying apple pieces quickly became the major activity of the ants. When the apples got too mushy, they started carrying chunks of dirt instead. The tiny creatures were in constant motion. The only ones not carrying were the ones on secret reconnaissance missions to the opening, where they would hide for hours waiting for us to open the slot so they could spring out. Between the endless carrying and the escape attempts, our farm was more like a forced labor camp.

What the ants didn't do was dig tunnels. We tried everything. Well, not everything—we never got right in there and helped them, although once I stuck a knitting needle into the sand to give them the idea. We even covered the bottom half of the box with black paper, which was supposed to trick them into thinking they were underground, I suppose in the subterranean kitchen of the enormous mole-people.

After a few days, something seemed to trigger in their microbe-sized brains, and at last they started to fulfill their role in the grand design of ant farming: dying. Ants were never meant to live in a clear plastic box with colorful cartoon farm designs. They are meant to live in the cupboard, like other disgusting vermin. Every farm produces a harvest, and it was soon clear that we were going to have a bumper crop.

Now we knew that the lifting was training them for their ultimate job, which was carrying dead ants. We never saw them actually eating the dead ones, but they did take them for rides. The entire farm was only 14 inches wide, but each dead ant covered several miles before disappearing without a trace.

And finally, they started digging tunnels. They created elaborate pathways through the sand, an entire subway transit system exclusively for transporting dead ants.

One by one, the ants died off. We started to root for our favorites, giving them names based on their identifying characteristics, although they all looked so similar that the only useful characteristic was "not yet dead."

Eventually we were down to our last ant, who spent his time walking back and forth with no one left to carry. One day he too disappeared, making us wonder who would eat the last ant, a tremendous gaffe in polite circles. So far, we have not sent away for any more. Instead, we are applying for farm subsidies in case the government will pay us not to raise ants.

In the end, my sister was right. We learned many valuable lessons from the ant farm, like how fruit liquifies and the reward for constant, hard work, which is death. We also get a little nervous now when gas company trucks show up and start digging tunnels in front of our house.

I only hope my sister's children learn as much from our next gift to them, a working pneumatic air-hammer with a built-in super-soaker squirt gun, batteries not included.

Back to the Basics

Here's some good news for people suffering from back pain: Thanks to the federal government, there's an excellent chance that your doctor won't do anything to make it worse.

Everybody gets back pain. It is so common that it affects 92 percent of the population at some time, with the other 8 percent getting it during other, off-peak hours.

Unfortunately, medical schools don't teach doctors much about common, everyday back pain. Up until a few years ago many of them were still using terms like "lumbago." In recent surveys, many people thought lumbago was a type of RV, while others believed it was a Polynesian party dance where you bend backwards trying to pass under a horizontal bar.

Because of this, a lot of therapy for back problems was based on common sense and guesswork. For years doctors have been telling people with back pain to rest in bed. If they didn't get better they were given pain medicine and muscle relaxers, and told to stay in bed longer, sometimes for weeks. This treatment was handed down from doctor to doctor, back to back, without anyone bothering to find out if it worked.

That's when the federal government decided to step in and, as it so often does, make everything clear. To solve this problem, the Department of Health and Human Services hired a team of back care experts, including doctors, nurses, osteopaths, chiropractors, and physical therapists. These people were selected because of the incredible conglomeration of their advanced learning, meaning they had probably all experienced back pain themselves from carrying heavy textbooks.

The approach immediately led to one remarkable breakthrough, namely doctors and chiropractors spending time in the same room ("the Back Room") without trying to kill each other. Somehow, probably through the use of sedatives and heavy leather restraints, they were able to work together, coming up with many interesting findings.

The panel reviewed all of the collected medical literature on back pain, probably the most intensive homework assignment of all time. Together they read almost 4,000 reports taken from important medical journals (*Journal Of Musculoskeletal Medicine*), textbooks (*Neurosurgical Care of the Back,* 1992), and morning radio playlists ("My Boyfriend's Back," the Angels, 1963).

What they found out was this: Most back problems get better on their own. More than 90 percent of people who hurt their backs are better within four weeks, whether or not they even go to the doctor.

They also discovered that many of the standard treatments for back pain, like traction, ultrasound, back braces, and steroid medicine, really don't help at all. And since most simple back pain gets better in four weeks, there was no reason for most people to have X-rays or expensive CT scans before then.

This makes the doctor's job clear. Now, when patients come for back pain, the important thing is to check for serious conditions like infections (which cause fevers), pinched nerves (sciatica), or signs of fractures (bones sticking out.) Without any of these signs, most patients will get better on their own, without specialized treatments or old doctor's tales.

Instead, doctors can help them focus on the things that do work. The study showed that simple medicines like Tylenol and ibuprofen can help, unlike narcotics or muscle relaxers that aggravate the pain by making you so goofy you run into a chair on your way to the bathroom. Back manipulation can, like Tylenol, temporarily relieve symptoms during those first four weeks, when most people get better anyway. (While this sounds like Christmas for chiropractors, there was no evidence that manipulation got people better any faster.) They even resolved the age-old question of ice versus heat, revealing scientific data that proves once and for all that either one is fine, it doesn't matter, whatever.

What does matter is exercise. Treatments done *to* your back are never as good as doing things *with* it. Putting people in bed, while it seemed like a good idea, was exactly the wrong thing to do. Exercising every day, like walking or swimming (the back stroke, naturally), works better than any medicine or treatment in getting people better and even preventing episodes in the future.

Thanks to the federal government, doctors now understand how to take care of patients with back pain, which is basically to leave them alone. We can now forget about old, useless treatments and instead look ahead to a new way to treat back problems, as documented in the popular orthopedic instructional film *Back to the Future*.

A Klingon Walk with Thee

Geographically speaking, Minnesota is no closer to the rest of the universe than other states, so it's a little surprising to find so many people here who speak fluent Klingon.

Minnesota has become a major center for Klingon activity here on Earth. With our long winters and unforgiving climate, people here have always taken their fantasy seriously. This is especially true for *Star Trek* in all of its various incarnations, and for Klingons in particular. Without active fantasy lives, many of us might not survive until spring. In fact, by February many people think living on a savage, brutal, war-mongering planet might be all right, just as long as it was warm.

It is only natural, then, that Minnesota should be the birthplace of *Good News for the Warrior Race,* the first translation of the New Testament into Klingon. The project is the work of Dr. Glen Proechel, a linguistics professor at the University of Minnesota, and his book is attracting attention from Trekkers everywhere.

As everyone on this planet knows, Klingons were first created to be the bad guys in the old TV show *Star Trek*. Back then, they looked remarkably like bit players from TV Westerns, generally humanoid with slightly greenish faces. The race has definitely matured since then. Over the years, Klingons have developed their own culture, language, and several rows of lumpy prosthetic ridges on their foreheads.

The Klingon language was invented for the Star Trek movies. It contains over 2000 words, not counting associated growls, lip smacking, and several forms of spitting. With an official dictionary and several instructional audio tapes (*Conversational Klingon* and *Power Klingon*), it has become incredibly realistic for a synthetic language.

Formerly a vicious and savage enemy, Klingons have now become our allies in the modern Star Trek universe. According to Proechel, we should now be ready to share with them the vision of life found in the New Testament, a vision based on love, faith, and dependence on a "great lord."

The Bible translation project was unveiled at PolarisCon 3, a science fiction convention held at a motel in Bloomington, Minnesota, in the shadow of the intergalactically huge Mall of America. The Megamall encompasses essentially the rest of Bloomington, resting amidst its parking ramps like an enormous flying saucer from a planet where the people are the size of giant redwood trees.

The convention was part of a month-long festival of Klingons in our state. It included a "Shopping in Klingon" demonstration at the Megamall, just before the annual week-long Klingon Language Camp, held each July in Red Lake Falls, a small town in the northwest corner of the state. As you might have guessed, Dr. Proechel is also the director of the Klingon camp, which, in an effort to promote cross-species tolerance, is held in a spot close to the borders of both North Dakota and Canada.

The Bible translation was a popular topic at the convention, culminating in a Sunday morning worship service held entirely in Klingon. The service was held in the hotel auditorium, with a simple stage, podium, and the same uncomfortable folding chairs we use here on Earth. Dr. Proechel passed out programs showing various prayers and their Klingon equivalents, and led the congregation through a few preliminary exercises in Klingon language skills. He then introduced three Klingons who were onstage to perform as the choir, all of them dressed in black leather and chrome, all of them looking angry to be out of bed.

After a shaky start of myriad technical difficulties—as if convention organizers were somehow able to fly in alien species from other worlds but unable to get the sound system working—the service began with a reading of the Lord's Prayer, in Klingon.

As written, Klingon letters look like shards of broken glass laid into rows and sprinkled with fingernail clippings. The writing is full of sharp edges and spikes, much like their outfits. When translated back into standard Arabic letters, it appears to be English that has been irradiated with a random capitalization ray, looking soMth'iNG LikE tHIs'.

Speaking Klingon is equally risky. The accent marks are pronunciation clues, marking sounds called "high glottals," which require you to make a noise like you are clearing secretions from all your nasal passages at once.

As though Klingon prayers were not inspiration enough, the worship service also featured the choir of Klingons singing hymns in their native tongue, an experience I can only relate to listening to a group of people drowning in a given key. There is no way I can describe the effect of hearing "Amazing Grace" as sung by Klingons, a race of people who have been known to accidentally tear each other apart during sex.

This is, in fact, a major problem with the whole Klingon Bible project. Familiar passages sound quite, well, alien when filtered through Klingon sensibilities. Jesus Christ was "a great warrior who died on the claw." A moving Bible passage like Matthew 5:14–16, "You are the light . . . " becomes "You are the nova in the galaxy, a meteor that cannot hide itself in the black hole." Faithful readers are reassured that "there is neither Ferengi nor Klingon in Jesus." Many of the New Testament parables deal with agricultural metaphors, which don't translate at all and must be replaced with military ones: "I am the Bird of Prey; He controls my deflectors and repairs my warp engines."

How else can you convey warm, loving messages to a people who believe the highest honor is death in combat, and who are, by the way, entirely fictional? Klingons have no words for love, faith, or hope. It is not easy to communicate the central message of Christianity, "God is with you," when there is no official Klingon word for "God," or, for that matter, for "with."

But of course, that's the challenge of going where no man has gone before. After the service, with the Klingons presumably back in bed, I did experience a sense of peace and understanding toward my fellow bipedal humanoids. At least someone is making the attempt to foster better interstellar communication. It was reassuring to know that even Star Trek fans recognize the need for a "vav Ma'," a supreme being and spiritual leader who is responsible for the creation of the entire universe—besides Gene Roddenberry, I mean.

And at least here in Minnesota we'll be ready to pass along the good word if actual Klingons ever do show up. Who knows? They just might want to do a little shopping.

Blood Tests for Vampires

As a doctor, I get asked a lot of medical questions. Luckily, thanks to regular readers, my office has become a regional clearinghouse for wacky medical news. All I need to do is match up the questions with the latest goofy medical report. This allows me to share important medical information and, more importantly, clear off my desk once in a while:

Q: Do you need a blood test for a marriage license?
A: Blood tests are no longer required in most states, although some places still use them to detect sexually transmitted diseases. They believe this is the perfect time because, as everyone knows, no one ever has sex before marriage. Actually, it might be better to test everybody else, since people getting married will presumably be out of circulation for a while.

Instead, at our large county office you receive a newlywed sampler kit, presumably to ease the transition into married life. It contains Secret-brand deodorant and Zest-brand soap, though applicants must already smell good enough to attract a potential mate, along with Cheer laundry detergent and Bounce-brand whatever-those-little-squares-are.

(Q: While people deserve every chance at staying married, does anyone think it's wrong for government employees to provide free advertising and promotion for a company like Proctor and Gamble?

A: "I do.")

Q: I'm thinking of going into politics, but I worry about getting struck by lightning when I start lying. Will this cause any side effects?

A: Yes, according to Dr. Hooshang Hooshmand (really, his actual name), a leading world authority on lightning injuries. He spoke at the fifth annual Lightning Strike and Electric Shock Victims convention, the only major international meeting where everyone has hair like Don King. Dr. Hooshmand says lightning victims need treatment and compensation for stuttering, memory loss, depression, blurry vision, and poor hearing, along with one guy who swears, "I haven't felt cold since 1969."

These claims are hard to believe because (1) the symptoms are all very subjective and hard to document, and (2) Dr. Hooshmand has already been convicted once for Medicare fraud. In this case, I wouldn't worry about it. While having 5,000 volts coursing through your body might result in poor judgment and brain damage, in politics these may be considered assets.

Q: The only way my kids encounter chickens is in nugget form as part of a Happy Meal. Do they need the new chicken pox vaccine?

A: Chicken pox vaccine has nothing to do with chickens, but everything to do with marketing. There are eight-page color ads in every parenting and doctor magazine touting the new vaccine. Drug companies know that there is little money in researching rare, scary diseases like Ebola virus, but if they can convince every parent in America to give their kids a shot for a common disease like chicken pox, they will make billions. Meanwhile, one in four children is still not vaccinated against serious infections like hemophilus, which causes meningitis.

Unfortunately, the vaccine doesn't usually prevent chicken pox, either; it only delays it until sometime later, probably prom night, when children are older and the infection is much more severe. So ask your doctor, but ask like this: "Should my child get an expensive vaccine with many potential side effects in order to postpone a common, self-limited illness until later when it will be much worse?"

Otherwise, you might want to wait. Judging by the massive ad campaign, it's only a matter of time until chicken pox vaccine comes free as a prize in Happy Meals everywhere.

Q: In the Tom Cruise movie *Interview with a Vampire,* being bitten by a vampire looks like fun. Are there any health risks?

A: You have to weigh the pros and cons: Yes, being bitten will turn you into a depraved, soulless member of the walking undead; on the other hand, it may lower your risk of having a stroke.

Scientists in South America have isolated a protein in the saliva of vampire bats that stops blood clots, which they have turned into a drug that might prevent strokes and heart attacks. They call it "Draculin," in honor of the head bloodsucker, who was not, interestingly, an attorney. It will be sold only at night. Thanks to science, there is now a way to get all the benefits of a vampire attack without being bitten by prissy, rouged, pretty-boy vampires like Brad Pitt.

Q: Are breast implants safe or not?

A: Recent studies show no connection between implants and serious disease. This means breast implants are not dangerous, only senseless and silly. Plastic surgeons are anxious to start installing them again, but bad publicity has forced the manufacturers to look for other markets for their product.

In Japan, for example, some teenage sumo wrestlers inject silicone into their scalps to reach the minimum height requirement for the sport. Breast implants could be easily adapted for this, although the teasing and nicknames from other teenagers would be brutal.

They could also be marketed as personal safety devices, thanks to the true story of an exotic dancer in Tampa who was shot at close range and saved from death when the bullet was deflected by her breast implants.

Q: Why are men so grouchy?

A: According to a story sent in by a local TV anchorwoman, some men are grouchy because they lack enough of the male hormone testosterone. There is a narrow range for normal testosterone levels in men—too little, and they get grouchy; too much, and they become aggressive and antisocial.

This is an important point for women to remember about testosterone, which now comes in an easy-to-dissolve tablet form that is virtually undetectable in beer. Otherwise, they could risk harming a loved one or, even worse, becoming the subject of a wacky medical story of their own.

Physicals Attraction

For a long time doctors believed that their patients would gradually grow old, become sick, and eventually die, unless they had annual physicals.

Are these physicals really a good idea? Let's take a closer look at the annual physical, dissecting its parts like a frog in a junior high science class:

"Annual"

For years, doctors told people to have annual physical exams. This started as an insurance company gimmick, without any proof that it helped people stay well. After a while, these physicals were considered regular maintenance visits. People started going to the doctor like they would go to Hasty Instant Oil Change, where crack teams of maintenance professionals go over your car with a fine-toothed, but greasy, comb.

Visiting a doctor is not like having your oil changed. For one thing, doctors rarely show you the parts they remove. And they don't communicate like a well-oiled team of service technicians ("Blood sample OUT!! Prostate CHECKED!!"). Your body doesn't need routine fluid level checks, which is lucky because you can't easily shut it off to look under the hood.

Women have traditionally been better at having regular physicals, mostly because they had to come every year for pap smears and birth control pills. Men are on a different schedule, having physicals whenever somebody forces them to go. At first this means parents, school nurses, and Scout leaders, but later they rely almost exclusively on their wives to send them.

Even married men, however, rarely get physicals. A recent survey showed that one in three men have not had a checkup in the last year. This amounts to 31 million American men, which sounds like a lot until you realize that we do this many school physicals in our office during the month of August alone. Their reasons for avoiding doctors varied—64 percent said it cost too much, 37 percent didn't have time, and 26 percent mentioned a particular scene in the James Bond movie *Dr. No*.

This survey was supposed to prove that men are feeble, helpless infants, but they may actually have the right idea. No one needs a physical every year. In fact, experts say that healthy people only need to come in every three years. For women, this is perfectly safe as long as their pap smears have always been normal. For men, they will stretch it out, stalling and whining, until five years have gone by, which is about right for them.

"Physical"

When having an annual physical, the "physical" part is probably the least important. Most people think that doctors can discover everything about you just by laying on hands. They can, but this is carefully regulated and I can't discuss it here.

The real reason to have a physical is not to find out if you are somehow secretly ill. Most diseases do not go undercover like foreign double agents, to be ferreted out by doctors using secret decoder thermometers and stethoscopes that shoot tear gas. Your body is much smarter than a CIA administrator—if an intruder is present, it will usually notice and give you some warning.

This also goes for blood tests. Doctors used to order forty different blood tests on everyone, including glucose, bilirubin, magnesium, riboflavin, porcelain, chlorophyll, cellulite, and so forth. Nobody can have this many tests and still have all normal results. The doctor then has to figure out why, which means ordering more blood tests, some of which will be abnormal, and so on. This quickly becomes the medical equivalent of a whack-a-mole game. Patients can find themselves having exploratory abdominal surgery because they forgot and ate a Snickers bar on the way to the lab.

This whole process is based on the notion that people are basically sick, they just haven't figured it out yet. The truth is that people are basically healthy. Rather than conduct a lot of unnecessary tests, doctors now focus on helping their patients stay that way.

Reminding patients to wear seat belts does more good than any blood test. Quitting smoking is more important than having a doctor listen to your heart and what's left of your lungs. A better diet can keep you alive longer. This is the "doctor as mother" approach, which relies on sound medical principles like these: "Don't eat so much. Stop that. Go on, get out, get some exercise, you're driving me crazy."

Checking on a few important things like blood pressure and cholesterol every two or three years does more good than having a complete physical every year. And with only a few items on the list, doctors can discuss them whenever they see a patient, even when they are just asking a medical question at the grocery store.

This lets doctors get back to important things, like taking care of sick people or watching old James Bond movies. That way, they can see at least one person who never gets old and will never die.

Doctors on the Bat-Line

With the health care field turning into a rough-and-tumble, no-holds-barred rugby game, many people believe it is doctors who are on the bottom of the scrum.

Salaries of high-powered specialists have been dropping like autumn leaves in a downdraft.

Not many doctors have their own practices these days. Most individual and small group practices are being sucked up like plankton into the belly of a Blue (Cross or Shield) Whale.

Giant corporations are now running the entire health care industry. More doctors are finding themselves as mere employees, who have to fill out forms to take vacation and might soon be forced to wear paper hats. ("Hi, welcome to McDoctors. Can I take your symptom?")

Many people wonder who, when faced with such bad metaphors, would ever want to be a doctor?

The answer is: "lots of people."

Applications to medical schools are once again on the rise, and there are people lined up waiting to become doctors.

Cornell University Medical College received more than seventy applications for each available slot. To make things worse, the administrators made the mistake of sending out more acceptance letters than they had spaces for new students. Most schools do the same thing, assuming some students will choose other schools or change their minds and become rug doctors instead.

Not this year. Their incoming freshman class has been overbooked like a cheap flight to Cancun. Medical school administrators are desperately looking for people willing to be bumped.

They are offering a pretty good deal. Anyone who agrees to defer until 1997 will receive free tuition for a year, worth about $24,000. Basically, they are having a sale—buy three, get one free. Anyone who acts now will also receive, at no additional cost, a free apartment in student housing for the entire year. They might even throw in a lovely set of ginsu knives, which will come in handy later during gross anatomy.

Despite the grim outlook, more people still want to be doctors. This is a result of the incredible amount of attention now focused on health care, the current instability in leading economic indicators, and, most importantly, the hugely popular television program *ER*.

The same thing happened to law schools during *LA Law*. TV has a profound effect on young people, especially when they see charming, heroic doctors like George Clooney saving lives, dating international starlets, and eventually getting to be Batman.

Actually, I think medicine is once again a popular career choice specifically *because* of the recent changes in health care.

Most doctors don't know much about running a business. They don't teach marketing or finance in medical school. Doctors don't know about business any more than insurance company administrators know when someone should go home from the hospital. (Hint: It's not "when they stop bleeding.")

At one time, doctors could afford to be in charge, not because they were any good at it but because it didn't matter. There was enough money coming in that they could afford to make a few mistakes.

Doctors on the Bat-Line

Now, with health care costs out of control, management principles like efficiency and cost control have become much more important, and doctors can no longer accept payment in nonnegotiable assets, such as small farm animals or cherry cobbler pie.

Working for a large company means giving up some autonomy, but at least doctors today don't have to worry about the business side of practice. They can concentrate on medicine.

New doctors coming in will be able to spend more time taking care of sick people. This is why many of them choose medical school in the first place. It is hard enough to keep up with the latest developments in medicine without trying to follow the unpredictable, tempestuous whirlwind of change in the health care field, possibly the worst metaphor of all.

This way every new doctor can look forward to building a rewarding and fulfilling career, right up until the day when all of their planning and hard work pays off, and they finally get their chance to be Batman.

Back-to-School Supplies

Every year the summer ends and, as any parent knows, the entire country enters the next season in the glorious, ever-changing cycle of seasons: back to school.

I love back-to-school time, because it gives me a reason to buy more crayons. This is the absolute truth: I have been buying new crayons every fall my whole life. Mostly, I just smell them. (It's OK—it says "nontoxic" right on the box.) Nothing smells as good as a new box of crayons.

When I was little I always had boxes of eight or sixteen crayons. Later we could afford the box of twenty-four or even forty-eight, but real status only came with the large sixty-four-crayon box, because it had a built-in sharpener. This is the best marketing device ever invented. It encourages kids to peel off the paper and carve away most of the crayon, using it up even faster than pressing really hard to get that shiny, glossy look.

The school supplied most of the other things we needed, including paper with actual chunks of wood in it and pencils the size of an Aqua-Lung. The only things we had to buy ourselves were (1) a compass, which was theoretically for drawing circles but more commonly used for impaling your hand whenever you reached into your desk, and (2) a protractor, which was used for international design studies, such as drawing "French curves."

I never had to spend a lot of money for school supplies until I got to medical school. Although we never really got a break for summer vacation, we would still buy school supplies every fall (scalpel, No-Doz, dead body, and so forth).

Things have changed. A recent report on TV news said that parents this year would spend an average of $353 to send a child back to school, as determined by the National Bureau of Unverifiable Statistics.

When I heard this figure, I assumed it included food for the entire year. My son is just starting kindergarten, so his back-to-school list is pretty simple: markers, crayons (a sixteen-crayon box only, to discourage status seekers), a glue stick (which is much less appetizing than the white lumpy paste we used), and round-edged scissors sharp enough to slice through either wet newspaper or soap suds.

Like kids in every grade, he also had to bring a box of Kleenex. This is because germs, like halibut, live in schools. Whenever you put thirty children together in one room, they quickly trade germs and catch colds, turning into waterfalls of contagious mucus. Then they go home and hug their parents.

The total for our list was much less than $353, but that's because he is young. Take a look at this list for the fourth grade: six pencils, No. 2 regular; one eraser, soft pink, rectangle, slanted ends; one Cray super multimedia work station, network ready; one box Kleenex.

My sources, mothers with teenagers in junior high and high school, tell me that $353 doesn't even cover the cost of the shoes. Kids today absolutely cannot go back to school without the latest model shoes by Nike, like this year's popular Air Perots.

Older kids also require the latest organizer technology, which they obtain by whining and promising it will help them get better grades. Most of this centers around something called a "Trapper," an item which has polarized the school system. Schools are openly divided between educators in favor of Trappers and those that, like wilderness preserves, ban them entirely.

Special note to parents: No matter what your child tells you, you do not have to spend the extra money for a Trapper with the famous Nike "swoosh" logo. No rule says your child has to be popular. They could always become team manager for the chess club, or the audiovisual aide who runs the spotlight during the homecoming dance instead.

By becoming hopeless geeks they will be perfect candidates for medical school. Then they can afford the biggest, best box of crayons around.

I myself now own a super-deluxe box of ninety-six. It includes colors that are not even found in nature, like "morose" and "ephemerald green." It comes not with a sharpener, but with a year's subscription to a sharpening service.

I can't wait until my cold clears up. I bet it smells great.

New Hope for Depression

There have been a lot of new research studies into the causes and treatment of depression, and the results are, well, depressing.

Depression, as most people know, is a serious disease that strikes several groups of people, including (1) astronauts on long, dreary space flights, and (2) everybody else.

A recent study of Russian astronauts showed that many of them suffer from depression on long space treks. American astronauts don't have much experience with this problem, because most of our flights are shorter. Shuttle missions last less than two weeks, the same timespan as the movie *The Right Stuff*.

The Soviets were regularly experimenting with the effects of prolonged space flight. They found that after a month most people experience "space fatigue," which causes anxiety, insomnia, and depression. During a record 438-day mission in 1995, one of the highly trained professional scientists stopped talking to crew mates because of petty disagreements, like stealing the covers and leaving the cap off the tube of processed, dehydrated roast beef.

Luckily, this problem didn't seem to affect Shannon Lucid, the woman astronaut who has spent more time in outer space than any other American, including Dweezil Zappa. After six months on the Russian space station Mir, she was still chipper, though she had plenty of reasons to be mad.

NASA tried several times to pick up Lucid, but between booster rocket problems, hurricanes, and a dog eating the launch plans, her flight was extended almost two months. Finally, she returned home to earth, where she found that a lot more of us were moody, irritable, and depressed.

People are getting depressed at alarming rates, and it's more than just being cranky. A new study from the World Health Organization (WHO?) says that mental illness will become the number one killer disease during the next century. By the year 2020, more people will die from depression, it said, than from auto accidents and heart disease, numbers two and three on the list.

The study urges governments to spend less money on rare infections like Ebola virus (which has been featured in so many movies and TV shows that it now has its own agent) and focus instead on preventing depression, which can affect us all.

Some scientists think they know one reason why. Another recent study has discovered a virus that may trigger depression in people, just like it does in animals. Scientists have found traces of Borna Disease Virus (BDV—the virus, not the underwear), which makes horses, cows, and cats act strangely, in the blood of people with depression. About 30 percent of people with mental illnesses like depression have evidence of the virus. In fact, when their blood is re-injected into rabbits, the rabbits started acting depressed as well, becoming distant and tired, with absolutely no interest in sex.

As if depression weren't scary enough, this latest news shows that it might be contagious.

Luckily, despite all the bad news, there are a few rays of hope on the horizon. New research has also uncovered several new treatments for depression, which might help to combat this modern plague.

Like magnetic hats. Researchers have shown that placing a

magnetic field close to the head can ease depression. It works as well as shock therapy, which uses jolts of electricity to trigger seizures that act as a "reset" button for the brain. These crude shock treatments are used only when other methods fail. Now there is another choice.

In trans-cranial magnetic stimulation, a magnetic coil is placed on the scalp, sending pulses directly to the brain. Two-thirds of the people in the study got better after five daily treatments. No one had any side effects, except for the people with extensive dental work who had trouble getting their mouths open afterward.

Another promising study showed the beneficial effect of Saint-John's-wort—the plant, not the skin lesion. This simple remedy has been used for years to treat depression and other problems. Unlike most folk remedies, it might really work, according to this report. The extract has now been licensed for medicinal use in Germany, where it has been used with fewer side effects than prescription medicines.

If it works, it would probably be a good idea for all of us to start taking it. Judging by the ominous increase in depression first identified in the WHO report ("WHO's on first"), we should all be wearing magnets and taking wort. We should probably keep it in a shaker on the kitchen table, using it like a condiment to prevent depression rates from climbing even higher.

Otherwise, we might soon see people like Ms. Lucid asking to go back into space again, just to get away from the rest of us.

Surgeon General-less

How long has it been? A year, maybe two? Time goes by so fast. One day you are practicing medicine in your own office, knowing that you have a surgeon general on your side, then suddenly, boom, you are on your own.

That's what happened when Dr. Joycelyn Elders, the last surgeon general, was fired for saying that having unprotected sex was worse, in a public health sense, than masturbation. This was considered sacrilegious by some members of Congress, who don't want people doing either one. These congressmen, anxious for a chance to embarrass the president, raised such a ruckus that she was forced to quit. This was ironic, because it was pretty good advice for a guy like Bob Packwood, who might still be a senator if only he had kept his hands to himself.

Dr. Henry Foster was nominated as a replacement, but unfortunately he made the serious mistake of completing his medical training, which included learning to perform abortions. The exact number became a topic of debate, although "greater than zero" was

Surgeon General-less

the figure that angered right-to-life groups. His nomination was terminated in the second trimester, and there have been no new candidates since.

Now some members of Congress, bothered by all this talk of safe sex and common sense, are trying to eliminate the job altogether. "The position has become a platform to advance a liberal and offensive social agenda that's out of step with mainstream America," according to Rep. Robert Dornan, R-Calif.

I am a doctor, and I take care of a small portion of mainstream America. Most of my patients believe in liberal causes like avoiding diseases and staying alive longer. The surgeons general have always been advocates for health, not politics. You might not always agree with them, but they have always been concerned only with the public good.

Technically, the job has no authority over other doctors. The surgeon general is the official head of the Public Health Service, which was originally a branch of the military. Because of this they have assigned ranks and wear uniforms, which is why Dr. Elders always looked like the lieutenant in the Tony Curtis movie *Operation Petticoat*.

Although other branches of the military are not known for keeping people alive, the Public Health Service is also charged with protecting the country. The difference is instead of guns and missiles they use immunizations and little wooden tongue depressors.

The surgeon general also has other important duties, like releasing the annual *Surgeon General's Report on Smoking*. This says the same thing every year: that tobacco companies are killing us faster than our enemies ever could. Without these stern warnings tobacco companies would still be advertising their deadly products on TV, instead of just in newspapers, magazines, billboards, stadiums, buses, benches, and convenience stores where children gather to buy Slurpees and baseball cards.

They also give a lot of speeches, talking about health and personal responsibility to anyone who will listen. In fact, this may be the most important part of the job: being a pest. The surgeon general is continually flying around the country giving speeches that make people uncomfortable. They are a nuisance because they are constantly bringing up things that people would rather forget.

This has always been their role. In 1946, Surgeon General Thomas Parran got into trouble for trying to say the word "syphilis" during a radio speech. He was trying to alert people about venereal disease, but being on radio he couldn't show any colorful anatomic diagrams to keep people interested, and he was cut off. Future hall-of-fame Surgeon General C. Everett Koop certainly knew how to be a pest. His constant harping about the coming AIDS crisis was very annoying, right up until it arrived.

Doctors in the community can't always speak out and say the things people need to hear. They have to worry about making people mad. A surgeon general who goes on TV to talk about sex is throwing herself on the grenade to save the rest of us. She gets in trouble, or even gets fired, but afterward it gets a little easier for other doctors to talk about these things.

Unfortunately, for now we are on our own. Doctors are floundering around without a surgeon general, waiting and wondering who, if anyone, will take the reins and start shooting off their mouth for the good of the country. It's been long enough. We need a new nominee, one who will speak out even when congressmen grow faint at the sound of a word like masturbation—as if congressional leaders had been doing anything else while the entire federal government comes crashing down around their ears.

Until then, the people in charge of the public health will be lost, wandering aimlessly without purpose, direction, or leadership. You know, kind of like the rest of the country.

Head Lice Aren't Nice

Not to alarm anyone, but the earth really is being overwhelmed by an aggressive, relentless infection, exactly as predicted in the popular best-selling book *The Hot Zone*. The only difference is, instead of a killer virus, it is head lice, and instead of destroying all human life, it is mostly just making it itchy.

Head lice are out of control. These pesky little creatures live on the scalp, and they normally surface once in a while whenever school kids share combs or wear each other's hats. (Head lice are only found on the head, unlike other varieties of lice which are found I'm not telling where.)

Whenever a child picks up a case of head lice it immediately causes a severe, intense itching in the scalp of his or her mother, even when she is in a different state. Even reading about lice makes your head feel kind of prickly. Moms freak out because they think lice are associated with uncleanliness, but anyone can catch them. Luckily, head lice are not dangerous, just inconvenient.

As my friend Julie, a nurse and mother, says: give me dangerous any day. You can protect your kids from mere danger. In the last year, head lice have become so contagious that there seems to be no way to avoid them.

For some reason, the usual medicines aren't working. There are now seven over-the-counter medicines for treating head lice, which in the past have always had the same effect on lice as a super-soaker squirt gun on the witch in *The Wizard of Oz.* These pesky creatures have somehow become immune to the usual treatments.

Not only that, but there are reports that lice are getting bigger. Either they are staying alive longer, growing up as they laugh off the effects of the medicine, or they could possibly be taking steroids. Soon anyone who finds a louse will have to remove it from their hair and wrestle it to the ground until help arrives.

Doctors know what to do when threatened with a dangerous epidemic, as shown in the movie *Outbreak,* which was loosely based on the book *The Hot Zone,* in the sense that they were both originally written in English. Like Dustin Hoffman in the movie, real doctors spring into action when infection is near, quickly commandeering army helicopters to fly around the country looking for a monkey.

Actually, the most important people in this defense against lice are not doctors, but phone nurses. They are the ones answering medical questions from the general public, and with so many lice-related calls for help, they are fast becoming the experts in the field.

Phone nurses can give callers up-to-the-minute advice on these new, more aggressive head lice. According to one health department phone nurse, if one medicine fails you should switch medicines and try again. You can also leave the shampoo on your head longer, although wearing it out of the house will make you look like a walking Q-Tip. They also recommend enclosing any hats or scarves in plastic bags before hanging them next to other people's clothing. (WARNING! This is not recommended for the actual scalp itself.)

And they are now recommending that every parent carefully go through their child's hair every day, finding and pulling off all of the little egg cases, or nits. This is why you need the monkey. You do this until the epidemic is over, or until the nits get so big it becomes like pulling medium-sized grade-A eggs out of a carton.

In desperation, people are also turning to older folk remedies. Julie, an intelligent woman, has been sending her children to school with a dab of coconut oil behind each ear. She believes this will repel lice, even though it might attract fruit flies. Kerosene, pine tar, hideous white rubber bathing caps with plastic flowers on the side—people will try almost anything to prevent the problem.

Well, almost anything. The next step is a drastic one, demonstrated by Sigourney Weaver in *Aliens 3*: total eradication, not of the lice but of the hair. Without hair there is no place for the bugs to hide, and removing the nits is as easy as polishing a chafing dish. Some teenagers already shave large portions of their heads in random patterns. Many of them would relate to the new head lice celebrity spokesperson Sinead O'Connor, who would go on national TV and tear up photos of parasites.

Otherwise, the creeping menace may continue, spreading out of schools and daycare centers to anywhere people bring their scalps. Beauty parlors will be vacant. Workplaces and businesses will have to maintain strict rules, urging top business executives to stop sharing combs and hairpieces.

All of which would make a pretty scary movie. Watch for *The Head Lice That Wouldn't Die,* possibly starring Dustin Hoffman in the title role, using the classic drama technique, "method itching."

I'm finished. Go ahead and scratch—you know you want to.

A Guide to Confusing Medical Reports

Science marches on! Once again, an exciting new medical discovery has completely contradicted everything doctors have been telling people for years. Naturally, it involves—guess what—cholesterol.

Scientists have discovered that healthy women taking medicine to lower their cholesterol are not really reducing their chances of dying from heart disease. The only thing that medicine gives them is a false sense of security.

This doesn't mean that they can stop worrying about cholesterol altogether. Having high cholesterol is still scary, making a heart attack much more likely. It's just that using medicine to fix it doesn't work.

This shows that heart disease, as Scott Adams says in his comic strip "Dilbert," is basically something you get from eating too many cows. (This is astonishing news to most people, who expected any

A Guide to Confusing Medical Reports

important, cow-related truths to come from "The Far Side" instead.) The only way to fix the problem is to reduce the total number of cows eaten. Doctors then divide this into the numbers of "good" and "bad" cows.

With this new study, there is now evidence that cholesterol medicine does not help women, children, people over seventy, or anyone who has not had a heart attack already. This could be good news, except, of course, for women who have been taking these expensive, bothersome drugs, putting up with the frequent side effects and blood tests because they thought medicine would protect them. All doctors can say is, "It seemed like a good idea at the time."

This kind of thing happens a lot in medicine. Experts disagree all the time. You have to remember to take each startling new medical report with a grain of salt, if not a fifty-pound bag of highway-grade chemical de-icer pellets. Otherwise, the constant flip-flopping can drive you crazy, making you eligible for another medical study, namely, "The Effects of Confusing Medical News on Mental Health and Aggressive Behavior toward Health Professionals."

To help people cope, I am presenting a reassuring, all-purpose "medical research disclaimer." It can help you through this latest news, as well as any future goofy research reports. Clip and save, to use whenever you run across bizarre medical stories that make no sense:

Many people became surprised (concerned / suicidal) when new medical research proved that using prescription medicine (Oat bran / Hostess Ding Dongs) to reduce cholesterol (blood sugar / toe jam) does not really prevent heart disease (stretch marks / the heartbreak of psoriasis) in women (humans / the cast of *Baywatch*).

It is important to realize that research studies (crude animal experiments / board games) are never the final answer. Doctors (clinical investigators / geeks with protective goggles) are constantly re-evaluating their methods (annoying habits / allergies), and they are bound to run into occasional discrepancies (little white lies / paid political announcements).

New studies are constantly being performed by researchers (unemployed graduate students / supermarket bag boys) using the

Are You a Real Doctor?

latest scientific equipment (really big microscopes / Thigh Masters). Through constant communication (ceaseless bickering / graffiti) they are able to assemble a broad picture of medical science (plate spinning / bad mojo), rather than focus on a single result (blind date / episode of *She's the Sheriff*).

Besides, many of these reports are really press releases (pre-game shows / aphrodisiacs) designed to titillate the media (media-large / xxx-large) before anyone has had a chance to prove or disprove them. These are only preliminary results (flimsy conclusions / dream sequences), and no one should make important medical decisions (treatment plans / weekend plans) based on news bulletins until all the facts are in (the fat lady sings / Rush Limbaugh skips dessert), despite what TV news doctors (pompous, empty-headed, coiffured, posturing dimwits / Rocky and Bullwinkle) say in their sensational attempts to boost ratings (their salaries / their Yahtzee scores).

Based on this, any woman (any man / Roseanne) should ask their doctor a few questions before taking cholesterol medicine (their pulse / their doctor's pulse). On the other hand, everyone (you and me / especially you and me) should consider changing their diet (eating habits / late-night refrigerator expeditions) to cut down on the fatty foods (grease feasts / coronary artery spackle) that make cholesterol such a big problem in the first place.

It's either that, or stop reading the news (staging the news / becoming the news).

New Ulcer Medicines Hard to Swallow

Finally, some good news from the world of medicine: It's a great time for a stomach ulcer, as if anyone needed any encouragement.

As seen on TV, several prescription ulcer medicines are now available without a prescription. Three of the most popular brands are already for sale, with more coming all the time. This happened when recent studies proved that a major source of stress for people with ulcers was taking time from their busy schedules to go to doctors. Now, instead of requiring a prescription, people may soon get the medicine free with a Double Burrito Del Grande at Taco Bell.

This has already started to change the way people treat their stomach problems. Let's say you (well, not you necessarily, but someone) developed ulcer-type stomach pain. In the old system, you would go to the doctor and get some pills, along with important advice on changing your diet, handling stress, and avoiding things that make ulcers worse, like caffeine, lawyers, teenage children, and having a job. The whole idea is to prevent the problem from coming right back once you run out of medicine.

Under the new system, you go to the store and get some pills. There is no advice, no stress talk, just a two-page package insert in tiny print warning you that this medicine should be used as directed by a doctor, despite the fact that you got it at a convenience store, right on the counter next to the Slim Jims and astrology charts.

When prescription medicines go over-the-counter, two things happen: (1) They lose some of the magical power and mystique that comes with a written prescription from an actual doctor, a placebo effect that is the only reason some medicines work at all, and (2) insurance stops paying for it. This comes from the old days, when people believed that nonprescription medicines were worthless, just because they were made from snake venom and ground-up fish scales.

Not any more. These new nonprescription ulcer medicines are basically weak, wimpy versions of the same products doctors have been prescribing for years. They still make the original versions in prescription strength, which is two or three times stronger. Because these new pills are weaker, manufacturers can only advertise them to treat heartburn, not true ulcers, as if no one would ever think of taking two pills at a time.

Luckily, people are more knowledgeable about their health these days, thanks to Lifetime cable TV and widely available medical journals such as *Redbook,* which each month features articles like "What Your Doctor Doesn't Know." Some people already know what to do when they get sick, and they don't need a pep talk from a doctor. They should have access to any medicine that might help them. Otherwise, it would be like selling power tools only to licensed carpenters.

Of course, other people will just take ulcer pills while eating pizza and chili and drinking double espressos. After all, taking a pill is much easier than changing your way of life. Naturally, drug companies wouldn't mind if you kept taking their pills forever. One of their ads even recommends taking the pills before eating any food that you know is going to cause heartburn. This is like spraying the ax with Bactine before hitting yourself in the foot.

While it will probably be a while before they have a chemotherapy section next to the foot powder at Walgreens, there are several other medicines now available without a permission slip from your doctor:

•Seldane—The folks who make this popular anti-allergy pill worked hard to get it approved for nonprescription use, citing important research that says everyone is already taking it anyway. This eliminates the need for the typical allergy appointment, which goes like this:

Patient: "I need more Seldane."
Doctor: "OK."

•Nicotine gum—These companies won FDA approval by arguing that cigarettes are already available so nicotine gum should be too, an example of backwards logic giving the exact wrong answer.

•Rogaine—Minoxidil, the famous "hair medicine," also went over-the-counter, a major breakthrough in preventing embarrassment in doctor's offices. (Special note to anyone considering this: C'mon, if this stuff really worked, do you think there would be so many bald doctors?)

Obviously, the do-it-yourself approach to medicine is here to stay. Someday, taking care of medical problems will be like remodeling your home. You could do it yourself, saving some money but leaving no one to blame when that beautiful new skylight comes crashing down on the new kitchen island, or you could hire an expert to do it for you.

Believe me, I know—you can do a lot of damage with a power tool.

Exercising Your Options

Anyone training for their local marathon needs to know the following: it's already full.

Marathons always fill up. Actually, they are often more than full. They are overflowing. There are always too many people willing to pay $35 to run twenty-six miles, roughly the same cost as taking a cab. Some of them plan to resort to tricks, like sneaking onto the course disguised as police motorcycles, TV sports reporters, or other inanimate objects.

Marathon officials hate this. They are afraid that having too many runners would overload the water stops along the way, where they give out water, which is free. You would think $35 would be enough to cover it. They could easily let a few more people in, especially since they will already have traffic blocked off and everything.

Why are so many people dying to run a marathon? Why would they beg for a chance at the pain, boredom, physical exhaustion, and bloody nipples that result from running for four straight hours and ending up back where you started?

Exercising Your Options

While exercise itself may not be much fun, researchers in sports medicine (doctors who never wear ties) tell us that there is no greater feeling in the world than the feeling of having exercised.

"Having exercised" is such a powerful reward that people will put up with almost anything to get it. This is certainly true at health clubs, where they make you pay hefty membership fees and wear spandex before you can even break a sweat.

Most of these people are not running marathons, but using exercise machines for that "having exercised" feeling. Some of them drive their cars three or four miles to the club to spend an hour riding an exercise bike. If they used real bikes they could just turn around and go home again once they got there.

While machines are incredibly boring, they can still provide that warm, inner glow from exercising, plus a few minor, incidental benefits like hardly ever getting sick and staying alive longer. Exercise helps almost any disease, including scary ones like heart disease, diabetes, and high blood pressure. Even in the worst-case scenario, if your appendix bursts during a workout you will be in much better shape when they expose your stomach muscles in surgery.

That's the reason doctors are always nagging people about exercising. (It's not for the warm, inner glow that comes from having nagged.) Exercise can be even more important than medicine. I have patients who would be better off if they came for their appointments and spent the entire fifteen or twenty minutes exercising right there in the little room. Of course, that wouldn't make me much of a doctor. It would make me a personal trainer, with my own line of exercise clothing and a workout show on cable access TV.

Running is great, but not everyone has to run marathons. Any kind of exercise is good for you. Just walking a few miles alongside the marathon route can give you the same results as marathon running, except for the nipples. For some people, just getting up and physically walking across the room to change the channel would be a big step.

There should be exercise machines to simulate these simple, everyday activities, like a dog-walking machine, where you walk on a treadmill while a mechanical leash periodically tries to yank your arm out of the socket. It could have settings ranging from Chihuahua to Jake, my friend Doug's crazed labrador who once pulled down and ate a metal fence. Houses should come equipped with large gerbil wheels in the family room, next to an upside-down bottle of drinking water with a bent metal straw.

So while your local marathon may be full because of important aquatic considerations, there's still plenty of room on the roads, sidewalks, pathways, health clubs, malls, or just marching up and down in front of your own personal TV at home.

As for me, I am always one of the lucky ones. On race day I get up early, lace up my shoes, and participate in my favorite sports activity: watching a marathon.

Don't worry—I'm bringing my own water.

My Doctor, Myself

I've been spending the last few weeks wrestling with a difficult problem: I have been trying to find myself a doctor.

I know that sounds easy, especially for someone in medicine. I know a lot of doctors here in our city. I even work with quite a few I consider excellent physicians, but it has still been a difficult choice to make.

I have never tried to find a doctor for myself before. I have never really needed one since I finished medical school. I have always been lucky enough to stay healthy, avoiding any serious medical problems, and I know enough about everyday illnesses to know most things get better on their own. Even now, I don't think of myself as sick. I just need some advice, and I guess that's when you need a doctor of your own.

If it had been a simple thing I would have ignored it for a while longer, but my problem is this: knee pain. For someone who likes to exercise, those two words can make their palms sweat. Some of us marvel at the wonders of the human heart or kidney, but for a runner, the knee is the greatest miracle of human anatomy. It is important in any sport, and can adapt to almost any exercise. Unfortunately, it is also subject to an infinite number of conditions that can cause pain and disability. Having a bad knee represents everything I fear about getting older.

I see a number of athletes in my practice, and I know how to take care of knees. I also know what a bad patient I am. I needed to find a doctor for two reasons: (1) to provide sound, objective advice, and (2) to have someone to blame in case my knee didn't get better.

With these things in mind, I started looking around for a doctor.

I first thought of making an appointment with an orthopedic surgeon. I had already done the simple anti-inflammatory-and-ice treatment, and had even started some physical therapy at home, so I figured I should move on to the next level of care. The only thing holding me back was my training in family practice, and my belief that primary care is always the best place to start. Plus, to be honest, I wasn't too happy about seeing any specialty with the word "surgeon" in the title. Not yet, anyway.

I started casually polling some of my family medicine colleagues, quietly checking out their interests and styles of practice. Were they interested in sports medicine, like I was? Did they prescribe drugs or physical therapy? Did they make people quit running? How quickly did they refer their patients to the orthopedic . . . surgeons?

It soon became clear that I was looking for someone who would handle this problem exactly like I would have. I was essentially looking for myself as a doctor, even though I had already determined that I was not the best person to take care of my knee. Like many physicians, I was having a problem giving up control. I was still trying to take care of myself, and I knew that attitude would make me a lousy patient for someone.

No wonder I haven't seen another doctor since I broke my arm in college. Even so, I should have realized that I need a physician. I do a lot of physicals on men my own age, and I tell them that regular screening tests are important. Don't I need to have a physical, too? Who do I think I am, Superman?

The answer, of course, is that I have been getting a continuing physical exam every day for the last five years, since I finished residency and started practice. If the slightest thing goes wrong somewhere in my body, I am the first one there with a stethoscope or a mirror and a flashlight.

Nothing slips by the physical exam I am constantly giving myself. I have taken a stress test for fun, and I have my cholesterol fractionation memorized. Where my own body is concerned, I have taken the screening concept to the height of medical surveillance.

This self-exam process began on the day I started medical school, although I can't really count the time before I knew what I was doing. In those days, every checkup I gave myself ended with the same diagnosis: I had whatever horrible disease we had just studied in class, and I was going to die.

Fortunately, I was able to cure myself by doing what medical students always do, taking two or three days of several different antibiotics until I felt better. I certainly proved the old adage to be true: Take care of yourself, and you have a fool for a doctor and a fool for a patient.

I try to keep that in mind, but while I have been looking around for a doctor, an interesting thing has happened. My knee has started to get better. At least, I've convinced myself that it has. Either way, I guess I'll keep doing what I've been doing for a while, putting off my search for a personal physician until I really need one. At the rate I am getting older, it might not take too long.

Stranger in Surgery

I was in surgery the other day. I say that casually, like I go to surgery every Wednesday, but it has actually been several years since I have been in an operating room. Over time I tend to forget what surgery is like, how different it is from what I do in family practice.

I went there to observe an operation on one of my patients, a young man with high blood pressure. The army had discovered the problem when he tried to enlist and sent him to me. During the next week I discovered that he had an adrenal tumor, one that was secreting hormones responsible for his sky-high pressure.

I called a surgeon, and we made plans for the operation. "I'd like to observe," I told him. He was a little surprised, but said he would be glad to have me. It would be a fascinating case, he told me with anticipation. He could use the help. I just hoped I'd be able to stay out of the way.

The morning of surgery I stood there in my green clothes, watching the patient getting scrubbed with orange soap, and I tried to remember the lessons on "How to Survive in Surgery" from my years in medical school.

Stranger in Surgery

First, stand near a pole. There are people buzzing around all over the room, running back and forth with drapes, gowns, strange-looking instruments, and who knows what else. Stay well to the side of the room, near a pole, and you won't get knocked over.

Second, keep your hands near your body and above your waist. The most popular stance is the "crossed arms on the chest." Variations include the "flat hands in the armpits" and the "Abraham Lincoln" stance, which is grabbing two handfuls of gown material up near your collarbone.

Finally, don't touch anything. Yourself, the furniture, anything. Wait until someone asks you to touch something, hesitate for a moment, and then touch it slowly, while watching their face to see if you have botched it.

As we got ready to begin, I was surprised by the crowd in the operating room. I think of surgery as a lonely job, but there were eleven of us—six sterilizing, two anesthetizing, two roaming around the room, and one unconscious and painted orange. It seemed like a lot of people, especially because they all knew their jobs so well and I felt so out of place.

One of the sterile people was a medical student. As the surgeons worked they would occasionally fire off a question at him. "What's the name of this maneuver? Is the condition bilateral? What are some associated conditions?" The student stammered and stuttered like I used to during this kind of barrage, and I had to smile under my mask. I didn't know the answers either, but that was one of the nice things about being a practicing doctor—nobody asks you those kinds of questions anymore.

For the next two hours I had to concentrate on one important task: not touching my nose. The instant I put on a mask my nose starts to itch like a bad rash. I don't know how surgeons put up with their noses, but I tried to ignore mine as best as I could, knowing the nurses would spot the slightest motion of my hand in that direction, and I would have to change gloves in humiliation. It had happened before.

As the operation progressed, I was amazed by the clean, precise incisions the surgeons made as they approached the adrenal gland. At every layer they gave special attention to any bleeding, making sure everything was dry before proceeding. If someone handed me a scalpel and an unconscious patient, it would be difficult for me to even find the adrenal glands, let alone be neat about it.

The surgeons soon exposed a large mass above the kidney. It was clearly the source of the problem. When they gently squeezed the adrenal gland, a monitor showed the blood pressure raising slightly. When they tied the final vein, removing the gland from circulation, the patient's blood pressure dropped precipitously. The anesthesiologist was ready, carefully monitoring the vital signs as he opened IV lines and adjusted dials. In a few minutes the pressure stabilized—at normal.

One of the surgeons reached over and set a gray lump of tissue on the tray in front of me. I found myself face-to-face with a pheochromocytoma, the tumor causing all the trouble. It looked small and powerless on the tray. I blinked, not used to seeing the enemy at such close range.

As they closed the incision, I thought about the hundreds of patients I have seen for high blood pressure and how each one had been controlled, more or less, by medication. This was the only time I had ever seen a case of hypertension cured once and for all.

The team backed away from the table, and one of the sterile people stapled the skin wound closed. I hurried to the dressing room to remove my mask and give my nose a good scratching.

I probably won't be going to surgery anytime soon, but it can be an interesting lesson for anyone in primary care. The operating room is a different world. Maybe we should all spend a day in surgery every once in a while.

Don't forget to stand by a pole, and for goodness' sake, don't touch anything.

Fertility, Guaranteed

Up until now there was only one guaranteed way to get pregnant, which involved a strapless evening gown, a wrist corsage, and the back seat of your father's car.

Not anymore. Doctors at several infertility clinics have started offering refunds to their patients who do not become pregnant. They will return their fee of $14,000 for in vitro fertilization, where egg and sperm cells are combined in a dish and later implanted into a woman's uterus, if a patient fails to become pregnant within three reproductive cycles, or, in technical terms, strikes. The doctors at these clinics estimate that about a third of their patients could receive refunds.

This $14,000 does not cover all the costs for in vitro procedures, such as the cost of the powerful hormone drugs, the intake screening charge, postage and handling, dealer prep, excise tax, and so on. The bill for drugs alone can be $2,000 a month, a huge expense for anyone who is not a major rock star. The screening charge is another $2,000, which is nonrefundable even when you are turned down for reasons like advanced age, illness, or bad fashion sense.

This is a lot of money, but infertility experts are working with a desperate population. There are not enough children for every loving family who wants one. Many people have to adopt highways instead. Infertility doctors offer the dream of natural childbirth, for a fee—a bundle of joy, for a bundle.

At the same time, the whole field of assisted reproduction has come under attack. A *Newsweek* cover story titled "The Baby Myth" showed that this was not really the miracle science portrayed in TV movies starring Jaclyn Smith. Nationwide, the odds of success for in vitro fertilization are not very good. In 1993, three out of four couples who went through infertility treatments did not have a baby afterward. In fact, no one has ever proved that new, high-tech fertilization procedures are any better than the one that was used seventeen years ago to conceive Louise Brown, the first test-tube baby.

Obviously, infertility specialists had to do something. It was either offer a money-back guarantee, or put enormous inflatable animals on the roofs of their clinics.

The idea of doctors giving refunds has some medical people worried. One doctor called the practice "worrisome as a trend in medical services," which is like saying the O. J. trial dragged on a bit. Regular doctors cannot offer refunds when things don't go well. The outcome in medical cases is not always something doctors can control. People get sick, doctors try to help them get better, and luckily, most of the time it works. Still, bad things can happen even when doctors do their best, a fact that eludes most malpractice lawyers.

But infertility is not really a disease. It affects normal, healthy people, who would not otherwise need help. Doctors who perform these treatments are not saving lives; they are selling a service. They are using their skill and medical technology to give people what they so desperately want, turning healthy people into patients in the process.

This is not a new role for doctors. The most common example

148

Fertility, Guaranteed

is in cosmetic surgery, where doctors routinely put price tags on body parts like noses and breasts. Operations like these must come with some kind of warranty. After all, when you show up for plastic surgery clutching a bag of money and a photo of Demi Moore, you darn well better look like Demi Moore when you leave.

Unfortunately, these same promises are being made to childless couples. Too many of them are taught that medicine can solve any problem. For them, no price will be too high, no procedure too painful or demeaning to try, even with such small odds for success.

Meanwhile, there are some not-so-small towns where they can't find doctors to deliver babies for people who are pregnant already. Cost controls and malpractice premiums make it hard to keep obstetricians in practice, especially when new mothers spend longer getting pregnant than they do on the maternity ward after delivery.

The fact that infertility doctors can offer refunds shows how lucrative this field can be. They can afford to offer rebates, keeping only a portion of their fees, and still make a healthy profit.

At least, until now. The next step is obvious: coupons. The day may come when you will get a coupon for a free baby when you buy a box of pampers, instead of the other way around.

Primary Care for Your Lawn

Summer signals the official start of the lawn care season, when many people enjoy lush, green lawns, unless, of course, they tried to do any actual lawn care.

It is a closely guarded secret of the lawn care industry, but many lawn care products are deadly poison to grass. I found this out when I bowed to neighborhood peer pressure and for the first time used a lawn care product, called "lawn food," on my yard. These products work remarkably fast, and in only a few short days my lawn was crisscrossed with long streaks of dead brown grass, as if someone had landed a stealth F-16 there during the night. Lawns are evidently like goldfish, gobbling up any last bit of food until you find them the next day floating belly up near the house.

Fortunately, I am sloppy. I missed long areas between the rows, and these are now the only areas of surviving grass. They are full, lush green stripes six inches wide, perfect for lawn bowling or worm races. The rest of the yard consists of large bald spots, which I cover using the popular method of letting the grass on one side

Primary Care for Your Lawn

grow really long and just raking it over. I'm sure no one can even tell.

As a male I am genetically assigned to the role of primary care provider for our lawn, but I believe you should never spend more time doing lawn care than you spend using the lawn. Unless you are careful, lawn care can easily take up all your Saturday mornings, when families should be spending time together watching cartoon reruns of The Tick. There are people who spend all summer trying to grow thick, green grass without any bright yellow dandelions, only to spend even more time planting other colorful flowers around the edges. Meanwhile, dogs everywhere are clearly working for the other side.

This is even more frustrating when you see beautiful green grass growing in places like along freeway exit ramps, which never receive any noticeable lawn care. Our local park skating rink, which is covered all winter with ice and fourteen-year-olds wearing sharpened metal blades, turns into a beautiful green landscape in about a month, with very little obvious work.

One of my partners has found a unique and exciting way to get out of lawn care. He performed a "prairie conversion" on his yard, transforming his entire lawn back into a more natural and environmental state. Naturally, this idea appealed to me. I am always interested whenever being lazy becomes politically correct.

Unfortunately, there is more to it than just letting the grass grow. It requires a lot of money and effort to re-populate a prairie. You have to use the proper kind of plants, which attract prairie wildlife to your yard, mostly to eat them. Then you have to buy more. This would be a part of "The Great Circle of Life" (Regis.™ 1994, Walt Disney Co.), except in the suburbs you can't kill and eat them back, like you would if you lived in a sod house on a real prairie. And there is the little problem of your neighbors, who are rarely big fans of Laura Ingalls Wilder.

The other method is to turn lawn care over to chemical companies, who will send big trucks to your house every month to spew toxic liquid on your yard. I worry about putting anything on my grass that requires a warning sign. There are case reports of small pets becoming confused and sexually infatuated with lawn furniture. I do not want to walk outside barefoot to get the paper only to come back drooling and wetting myself.

Obviously, lawn care can be not only frustrating and time consuming, but dangerous. If you really need the warm inner glow that comes from living near a perfect green patch of yard, consider Astroturf. This is the lawn care equivalent of a really bad hairpiece, like the ones on late-night TV ads for "The Lawn Club for Men." I'm sure no one will even be able to tell.

Keeping Up with Medical Breakthroughs

Every year there are so many amazing medical advances that most people could never possibly hope to keep up.

Fortunately, as a trained medical person, I am able to keep the finger of my alertness on the burgeoning pulse of medical research. Each day I scour the latest newspapers, medical journals, and TV talk shows in an effort to keep up with the latest startling developments, just so I can make fun of them here. No, don't thank me—it's my job.

•For the first time, women now outnumber men in medical school classes at both Harvard and Yale. This will lead to significant changes in years to come. We'll see who'll be taking the birth control pills then.

• Insurance companies have started limiting the amount of time new mothers can spend in the hospital after delivery. This was supposedly done to cut down on infections—hospitals are, after all, full of sick people—but coincidentally will save insurers millions of dollars. Next year they plan even shorter stays, eventually leading to maternity drive-through windows. ("That will be $2,000, please. Cut your cord and pull ahead.")

Naturally, these decisions are all made by men, who have no idea what it feels like to deliver a baby. Women know that any male who passed a seven-pound object through his own reproductive organs would be in intensive care for months, besides receiving years of therapy afterward.

• Scientists have discovered a new treatment for serious skin infections: maggots. Live maggots are very good at removing dead and infected tissue, and they can sometimes heal contaminated wounds when expensive medicines fail. So far, nurses are having trouble with the bandage changes, which have to be done before the therapy pupates and flies away.

One main disadvantage is that maggots are cheap, easy to produce, and cannot be patented. This means that drug companies could never use them to gouge the public with obscenely high prices. They could not even afford flashy ads in doctor magazines and cable TV, starring celebrity spokes-fly Jeff Goldblum. Until these bugs are worked out, the only place in large pharmaceutical companies for disgusting vermin will continue to be the boardroom.

• Researchers have finally discovered a treatment for the heartbreaking problem of chocolate addiction. Naloxone, a drug used in heroin treatment, has been shown to block the craving for chocolate that occurs primarily in women. (Men usually crave foods high in fat and salt, which go much better with beer.)

The drug blocks production of the specific brain chemical responsible for pleasure. This helps control cravings that trigger chocolate binges following blind dates and dismal, weepy movies

Keeping Up With Medical Breakthroughs

starring Meryl Streep, even though no connection between pleasure and Meryl Streep has ever been established.

Unfortunately, the medicine is only available in intravenous form. This makes it impractical, requiring you to shoot up in Fanny Farmer before the cravings become too strong.

•Baseball legend Mickey Mantle proved that he was still an important sports figure as he set a new world's speed record for acquiring a transplanted abdominal organ. Mantle received his new liver after only two days on the waiting list. Most people wait months—the average is 142 days—and some die before their number is called. Doctors say no rules were broken, but that "it took the same amount of time it would take for any celebrity alcohol abuser."

Sadly, he soon died anyway. His doctors forgot to read the installation manual, which clearly recommends checking under the hood for other problems, like cancer, before wasting a perfectly good replacement part.

•Tobacco companies were dealt a stunning setback when they were forced to recall more than a million defective cigarettes. A manufacturing mistake caused smokers to feel dizzy and lightheaded. Ironically, these might have been the safest cigarettes ever produced, because anyone who gets dizzy might stop smoking before their eventual heart attack.

Now things are back to normal. Smokers are still getting dizzy, but only later when someone accidentally steps on their oxygen tubing.

•Scientists developed a new technique for transplanting human cartilage cells. Having way too much free time, they quickly used it to grow a living human ear on the back of a mouse. "This could be an excellent way to produce new replacement parts," said one scientist in a high, squeaky voice, providing good news for celebrity ex-ballplayers everywhere.

•And finally, a depression drug, clomipramine, was discovered to have an unusual side effect when patients taking the medicine, both men and women, experienced an orgasm every time they yawned. It is easy to see how this would help depression, even with the added dry-cleaning expense.

So far, it has been difficult for patients to get prescriptions for the medicine. Most of the available supply has been tied up by scientists staying up late performing important research testing.

As a dedicated medical commentator, I have made a thorough study of the problem. Unfortunately, only a tiny fraction of the population experiences this unusual side effect, and it doesn't—I mean, it probably wouldn't—work for me.

Virtual Colons

Not many people know this, but there are doctors out there working day and night in a concerted effort to help you get out of unpleasant medical testing.

Researchers at the Mayo Clinic in Rochester, Minnesota, have come up with a new way to test people for colon cancer. This is great news, because the old way was extremely gross. Up until now, the only sure way for doctors to check for cancer was to take a look inside the colon, a procedure that can be painful, expensive, and just plain icky.

For years, doctors have been telling people over fifty to have this test, called colonoscopy, but less than half of them do. Even doctors are reluctant to have it done on themselves. When I was a student doctor, the leader of our residency program taught me to recommend the test to anyone over fifty years old. Then he reached fifty himself. On his birthday the threshold suddenly became fifty-one, followed by fifty-two the next year, and so on.

Unfortunately, this means many people go unchecked. Colon cancer is the number two cancer in the country, killing about 50,000 people each year. It is second only to lung cancer, which is still in first place, thanks to the lobbying and marketing efforts of tobacco companies. In a way, this makes colon cancer seem even scarier, because there is no way to prevent it. The only hope is to discover it early, when treatment will help, and that means having the test. The only consolation is that most people only need to go through it every five years, while doctors get to do stuff like this every day.

That may change. The new, improved test uses a special CT scanner and new, improved computer technology, without any uncomfortable or unpleasant side effects.

Naturally, this is good news for doctors, who are mostly males. Like most men, they always want the newest, fastest, most advanced computers they can find. Men are continually inventing reasons, like "home finances," to justify buying new computers. They believe faster computers will allow them to be more productive, taking much less time to finish a game of solitaire.

Doctors will trade in those old, slow, bulky CT scanners in a minute, especially if it means having another remote control. Men measure happiness by the number of remote controls they have lying around. I'm sure radiology offices have twelve or thirteen different remote controls on the desks, surrounded by technicians who are trying to figure out which button controls the one-touch split screen freeze-frame on the MRI scanner.

It's not their fault. No one could possibly know how to run all those machines. The instruction booklets are always in broken English, with little stick figure diagrams that show how to position patients and sprint from the room. Walk into the basement of any major hospital and you'll see expensive, high-tech electronic devices with glowing neon numbers in the little window blinking "12:00 . . . 12:00 . . . 12:00," just like my parents' VCR.

Thanks to this new technique, colon cancer screening may one day be as easy as having a portrait taken at ProEx. The new test is easier, cheaper, and even better at detecting cancer than the old one. New software developed at Mayo can detect even tiny growths inside the colon. It also processes the data much faster, and is compatible with Windows 95. If you thought lawsuits were a problem

Virtual Colons

before, wait until anyone logging onto the Microsoft Network automatically has his or her colon examined.

This all points to the day when doctors no longer need to examine us, just scan us with a handy medical computer—that day being September 8, 1966, when Dr. "Bones" McCoy first waved his flashbulb over a Star Trek crew member and made the diagnosis, "He's dead, Jim." With better and faster computers, modems, and home scanners, we will someday have complete medical examinations over the phone. This will lead to better medical care, and to detailed, color graphic images of our internal organs being available for downloading on the World Wide Web.

Meanwhile, people over fifty should still have the older test done, at least until the new one is available outside the Rochester area. Sure, it may be unpleasant, but it could save your life. And remember, although doctors haven't quite come up with a painless, effective way to examine your colon, at least they're looking into it.

Waist Not

A new government study has shown that we are, as a nation, a bunch of fatsoes.

The U.S. Department of Agriculture recently released a report entitled *What We Eat in America,* another example of bureaucrats using your tax dollars to bug you. In the study they interviewed more than 5,500 people across the country to find out exactly what they ate in a two-day period.

This study took hundreds of hours and thousands of dollars to find out what we already know from walking into any fast-food restaurant. While many of these places now offer healthier choices, take a good look at the salads in the display case. Some of them look like they were made during the Reagan administration, when the qualifications for vegetables were pretty loose. They might even be plastic replicas of actual salads. Meanwhile, every single employee in the place is constantly busy making more French fries to put under the sun lamps, where they never sit long enough to even get a tan.

Despite this, the study showed that people today are eating less fat as a part of their total diet, with only about a third of their total calories coming from fat. The bad news is that this is true only because they are eating a lot more calories overall.

This wouldn't be so bad if these extra calories were going somewhere. They're not. Apparently, the fitness boom has more to do with Lycra spandex than with exercise. Most people wearing Nikes never exercise, with only one in three doing any kind of regular activity at all.

So even though people are eating less fat, they are getting fatter anyway. A third of the adults in the study were overweight. In fact, the average person was eleven pounds heavier than in 1978. While some of these people were undoubtedly "big boned," most of the change has to do "with what we eat in America": basically, whatever tastes good.

Many of these people must have fallen for the myth of fat-free food, which goes like this: "Hey, it's fat free—what can it hurt? I can eat all I want, starting with this entire fat-free pound cake." Unfortunately, fat free does not mean calorie free, as demonstrated by the burgeoning national waistline.

Now food scientists are ready to play another trick on us. Olestra is here, a new fat substitute that promises to make us bloated, nauseated, and vitamin deficient, but skinny. Olestra provides the good taste of fat without being absorbed by the body. This is because it is not technically food. The effect is exactly like drinking mineral oil, a major ingredient of many laxatives. With Olestra, eating potato chips will be just as much fun as the time someone put little squares of chocolate Ex-Lax in the candy bowl at the junior high dance.

There are a lot of booby traps like this waiting at supermarkets, but there are no short cuts to healthy eating. You have to use common sense. Instead of falling for new high-tech, chemically engineered snack foods, people would be better off eating things that have always been good for them, like fruits and vegetables. According to the What We Eat study, half of the people said they eat no fruit at all, unless you count Life Savers and grape-flavored Robitussin. And almost nobody ate enough vegetables, especially the dark green and yellow vegetables (the "repulsive" group).

If they did, maybe the national weight average would improve. Then we wouldn't have to depend on the government to institute a program like Daylight Savings Weight, where we all set our scales back eleven pounds.

Of course, everyone has to rely on fast food at times, especially parents of young children, who often select a restaurant based on the Happy Meal prize of the week. Watch out for tricks there, too, like "super-size" meals. While it may seem like a bargain, getting twice as many French fries for the same amount of money is not really a good deal.

And, while you're there, consider some of the healthier choices. Remember, if you pile on enough fat-free dressing, even the plastic salads can taste good.

HMO Knows

There has been a lot of talk recently about Health Maintenance Organizations, or HMOs, being, well, not very healthy.

People are worried that these insurance plans are putting profits ahead of medical practice. Some HMO doctors make more money when they do less for their patients, which leads people to believe that these doctors are denying procedures or medicines because they are too expensive. Some complain that HMO rules gag doctors, preventing them from even telling patients about certain costly treatments.

Some of them go further, believing that doctors and HMOs are in a conspiracy against their patients, even though that would leave no one left to pay the premiums. This turns the entire field of health care into an Oliver Stone movie.

The truth is, I never know what kind of insurance my patients have. This is not something I avoid knowing on purpose. I just can't figure it out.

Here in Minnesota, most doctors do not work exclusively for an HMO. Like many of them, I work at a clinic that accepts many different kinds of insurance. About half of our patients are on some type of HMO plan. Each plan has a different code on the billing sheet in the front of the chart. I have been a doctor for ten years, and I still have no idea what all these various codes stand for.

Health insurance is constantly changing. I never know when Health One Preferred Gold Choice changes its name to Medical Gold Preferred One Select, becoming a code Q instead of W. People are regularly forced to change insurance companies. I have patients who have changed plans every year; they have a different code each time I see them. Believe me, it is hard enough to keep up with new developments in medicine without trying to ride the whirlwind of the health insurance industry.

Luckily, this does not affect the way I do my job. Because I have no idea what kind of insurance people have, I end up doing the same things for everyone, no matter what coverage they have.

Sometimes this causes a snag. Occasionally I get a call from a pharmacist telling me that a particular drug is not covered by a patient's insurance, but there is almost always a similar or related medicine that will do the job as well, one that will be covered under his or her plan.

Despite the scary stories about HMOs turning down exotic treatments like bone marrow transplants, in primary care this is rarely a problem. If insurance doesn't cover something, it usually means there is a better, or at least cheaper, alternative. Drug companies are constantly dreaming up expensive new pills for the same old problems, even when the old ones work just fine. They want people to rely on medicine to fix any problem, even nonproblems like hair loss and wrinkled skin.

Insurance plans generally won't cover a treatment until someone proves it is worthwhile, or until local legislators step in and demand coverage so they can look good on the evening news. They pass bills mandating an extra day in the hospital for new mothers or prostate blood tests for everyone, even women, while thousands of families who don't have insurance are going without even basic health care like immunizations.

Thanks to my problem with codes, I think I might have inadvertently come up with the best health insurance advice when dealing with doctors: Don't ask, don't tell. There is no reason your doctor needs to know what kind of insurance you have. To diagnose or treat your problems, doctors should always recommend the best and most cost-efficient therapy that they believe will help.

Then the insurance details can be left to the people at the front desk. They're the ones who need to know. They understand it all much better than I do, especially since they are the ones with the secret insurance decoder rings.

"Not knowing" may be the best way for doctors to deal with health insurance. It keeps the medical and the insurance questions separate, and lets doctors practice medicine without being influenced by their salaries or by their HMO plans.

Otherwise, everything gets all jumbled together. Pretty soon we would see even more medical decisions being made by insurance adjusters, or, even worse, petty bureaucrats. This is much more likely to gag doctors than anything an HMO can do.

A Nose for Nicotine

When the FDA approved the new nicotine nasal spray, it took less than twenty-four hours before people started calling their doctors to ask for some.

This is scary. The magazine ads were not even out yet. This means big trouble for me, especially when I tell people I am not physically able to prescribe it for them.

With gum and patches already available, you can now put nicotine into your lungs, your skin, your mouth, and, finally, your nose. Drug companies spend millions of dollars coming up with new ways to get nicotine into your body, as if they had already run out of diseases. This is to help people quit smoking, a feat that is nearly impossible because nicotine is so addictive. Scientists believe that the only way to simulate the incredible addictive power of nicotine would be if you could somehow convert daytime soap operas into IV form.

It is hard to understand how the answer to nicotine addiction can be . . . more nicotine. The theory is that these other products will take the place of cigarettes. You can then say that, technically, you have quit smoking. It's like that line in the Woody Allen movie: "I used to be a heroin addict; now I'm a methadone addict."

Of course, sooner or later you run out. Then you spend the next two weeks going through nicotine withdrawal, making you anxious, shaky, depressed, and as irritable as a wolverine with an ingrown toenail. This is why four out of five smokers are unable to quit for long, whether or not they use other nicotine.

According to the manufacturer, there are a couple of potential side effects with nicotine spray, including (1) an unpleasant stinging sensation inside your nose, and (2) death. We're not talking about Binaca here. Nicotine can cause serious problems, even if you don't accidentally squirt it in your eye. One little bottle of the new spray contains twice the lethal dose of nicotine, more than enough to make someone stop smoking permanently.

This is why I have a problem with nicotine. I just can't bring myself to prescribe something so horribly bad for you.

It's hard enough to prescribe medicines that might do some good. Doctors are trained to carefully review the side effects and possible interactions for any prescription drug, and even then, problems sometimes happen anyway. Even a medicine like Amoxicillin has a two-page instruction sheet describing all the things that could go wrong.

Nicotine has no good uses. The only reason to prescribe it in any form is to prolong a dangerous addiction. This makes doctors accessories to the crime, making their Hippocratic oath seem hypocritical instead.

I can't do it. When someone asks me to write a prescription for nicotine my hands start to shake, I get sweaty and nervous, and I am crabby for days afterward. I'm sure they leave the office thinking I am hoarding the medicine for myself.

This same thing would happen with the FDA plan to regulate cigarettes. How could any doctor write a prescription for such a deadly product? Doctors are always worried about getting sued, even when they haven't done anything wrong. Imagine how a malpractice lawyer's eyes would light up at the sight of a signed prescription with the word "Marlboro."

Are You a Real Doctor?

Actually, this might be the best plan. If cigarettes were regulated, doctors would not prescribe them, and sales would plummet. The entire country, smokers and nonsmokers alike, would have a really bad two weeks, with everyone acting unbelievably mean and ornery (except for Bob Dole, who would notice no change). Then it would be over, and I wouldn't have to worry about prescribing nicotine ever again.

Of course, judging by the current trend, by then we will be buried in new products, like nicotine shampoo, nicotine eye drops, and nicotine breakfast cereal.

Luckily, these don't require a prescription, so no one will call, and I can get back to watching my soap operas in peace.

Germs by Mail

It seems like people always have a lot of questions about new developments in medicine. Whenever I am out with my family at a store or a restaurant, someone will invariably come up to me and ask a question about medicine. I guess it's probably the white coat.

If one person has a question, then maybe a lot of other people are wondering about the same thing. And if four or five people ask me questions, then maybe, just maybe, I can turn them into a column, like this:

Q: I know you get sick by catching germs from other people, but where do the other people get them?

A: Mail order. There are several commercial suppliers who will send you biological cultures of many disease-causing organisms by mail. This is so scientists can obtain samples of these diseases to study, or, alternatively, to use as weapons of mass destruction.

A white supremacist in Ohio was arrested after ordering a culture of deadly plague bacteria. Luckily, he was captured before he could use it to infect the population, or, even worse, offer it for resale on the QVC home shopping network.

Are You a Real Doctor?

Now the government is considering tightening the rules. This makes sense, considering that under current laws you cannot buy lawn darts but can order anthrax by mail. Thanks to Congress, soon anyone placing an order for a disease-to-go may have to produce a note stating they are not an international terrorist.

Luckily, this legislation should pass easily. Unlike tobacco, most diseases don't have highly paid lawyers willing to argue that, for example, bubonic plague does not really cause any harm, or that while the plague killed almost half the population of Europe in the 1600s, no one ever conclusively proved the rats were to blame.

Q: Are car phones safe?

A: They are perfectly safe, as long as the car is not moving. A recent study showed that the chances of having an accident go up by 34 percent when you use a phone while driving.

The study also showed that those accident rates double when you are doing something else at the same time, such as eating while talking and driving. This goes against the popular belief that any food ordered from a drive-through is meant to be eaten in the car.

And, in a startling discovery, the study found that the risk of an accident is three times greater when you take both hands off the wheel. This is the kind of astonishing revelation that shows how medical research can change lives, proving conclusively that you are more likely to crash when no one is steering. I'm sure all of you will want to call your doctors and thank them. Wait until you get home.

Q: How can I get in touch with Dr. Jack Kevorkian?

A: Unfortunately, Dr. Kevorkian now has an unlisted number. You could call his old number, which now belongs to a woman in Detroit, but don't be surprised when you get a busy signal.

Since receiving the number, the woman's phone has been ringing constantly. For years Kevorkian advertised for his services in the classifieds section ("End of life planning. Equipment provided. Legal rep. a must") and people still call looking for his help. It got so bad she had to call the phone company to get "kill waiting."

The calls increase every time Dr. Kevorkian is acquitted. This is now so easy for him that he comes to court in goofy costumes or with one lawyer tied behind his back.

Sadly, this shows that there is a tremendous demand for this kind of service. Meanwhile, legislators are making it harder, not easier, for people to do it themselves.

Q: Did the University of Minnesota Medical School really lose $23.5 million dollars over the last six years?

A: If that were true, it would mean that the medical school is run by incompetent dimwits who have no earthly idea of how a medical school should work.

The truth is that the medical school lost that amount *in six months*. This is beyond belief. It is incomprehensible how any organization could go through this kind of money without its own space program.

As with every scandal-du-jour at the university, the problem has nothing to do with teaching students. Officials blame the changing medical climate. Very few doctors use the university as a source of specialty care anymore because it is inefficient and much more expensive than using other medical specialists.

Even so, the students are the ones paying higher tuition to make up for it. You just know administrators will be coming up with other suggestions for students, like re-using old textbooks from before the discovery of costly X-rays, or having students practice dissection on each other to avoid costly cadavers.

Otherwise, for that kind of money they could just close the school and give every incoming freshman student a one-time cash payment of $100,000 to forget the whole thing and get a job at Pizza Hut instead.

Q: Is sex dangerous?

A: There is no question that, given the current rates of sexually transmitted disease, sex is a scary proposition at best.

Still, it could be worse. Scientists have discovered a species of worms in which the mere act of mating shortens their life span by

50 percent. Granted, their life span is only seventeen days anyway, making it hard to develop any kind of long-term relationship.

All I can say is this: if you are thinking about having sex, try to protect yourself, practice safe sex, and try not to be a worm.

The Big Bird Doctor Kit

When my nephew turned two years old I wanted to get him a special gift. I bought him a doctor kit.

I'm not exactly sure why I chose it. My sister accused me of trying to push him into medicine, but that is not true. I would never try to convince anyone to be a doctor. It's not an easy job. I like it, and I am very happy, but it is not for everyone.

Like any two-year-old, my nephew has been to his share of doctors. Between ear infections and other simple problems, he has seen most of the stuff in his doctor kit before. Now, though, rather than be afraid of these things, he will get to use them on somebody else. As any doctor knows, this is much more fun.

There was a lot of stuff included in the kit. There was a stethoscope, one that actually works, sort of. At least you can hear something that sounds like it might be a heartbeat, that is if you can get the big blue ear pieces to stay in your ears without sliding into your nose.

There was an otoscope with a blunt end for safely checking ears. This was one of the reasons I got him the kit, so he could see that there is nothing scary about an ear light. Of course, this one has no light, but I think he'll get the idea.

There was a hard plastic reflex hammer that looks like you could use it to drive a railroad spike through a two-by-four. His mother sensibly put this away before he could start testing the reflexes on some of the other kids at his birthday party.

There was also a blood pressure cuff with a dial that spins when you squeeze the bulb. Of course, if the dial spun around like that while I was getting my own pressure checked I would be very worried, but my nephew seems to like it.

There was an eye chart, with several lines of large, colorful letters that spell nonsense words.

There were a few curved plastic Band-Aids that fit around a small arm or leg, nicely protecting the site of any "owwie."

There was also a "shot," sort of a nonthreatening version of a syringe. A small window fills up with red medicine when you turn the knob. The plunger moves in and out, but there is no needle. In fact, there is nothing in the whole kit sharper than a banana, which makes it pretty safe.

All of this comes in a nice blue doctor's bag with a picture of Big Bird on the front. I thought it was a pretty neat gift, and I was surprised how much stuff was in there. After we started to play with it, though, I realized there were a lot of things that, like batteries, were not included. They really should have put in a few more items to give kids a better idea of what being a doctor is really like.

For starters, there was no telephone. I don't know how many times I pick up a phone each day, but it is probably at least as many times as I use an otoscope, and many more times than I give anyone a shot. Of course, it would have to be a cellular phone, which all doctors now have. I like to have times when I can't be reached by phone, but I seem to be the only one who feels that way.

There was no coffee cup in the bag, either, and no snacks to keep in your desk for the times when you end up working through lunch.

There was no license or DEA number. These little scraps of paper mean little to me but seem very important to pharmacists.

The Big Bird Doctor Kit

There were no insurance or workman's comp forms. I assume these start appearing in the mail each day once you start using the kit.

Even more importantly, there was no nurse. I don't think I could be a doctor without a nurse to help me; they do all the real work. They bring in the patients, make them comfortable during the exam, help me order the proper tests and make sure they get done, and let patients know the results, all while directing the constant flow of traffic through the three or four little rooms where I spend most of my day.

For that matter, there was no receptionist included, either. And no medical records person, and no transcriptionist. And, as much as I hate to admit it, no administrators to help run the practice. I checked the box again, but no, they were clearly missing. Obviously, there were more things in a real doctor's kit than you could easily fit into a blue plastic bag.

Still, he was off to a pretty good start. At least his doctor kit will show him what it's like to take care of people. And if he decides that he likes the feeling of carrying around a doctor bag, well, nobody can blame me.

When Doctors Get Sick

I hate it when I get sick.

I bet all doctors do. Even a simple cold upsets me. It's not the congestion, the aching, the fever, or the uncontrollable coughing as much as the knowledge that I probably have something much worse.

Most doctors have this same fear, even if they don't talk about it. We learned it in medical school, where we all developed whatever disease we happened to be studying at the time.

I used to stay up until 3:00 A.M. studying, but when I was tired in the morning I knew it was because I had somehow caught mononucleosis from my textbooks. I rarely had time to exercise, and when I did I decided my lack of endurance was only the first sign of heart failure. During summer I was never tanned, but jaundiced. If I woke up at night I had malaria. If I slept straight through I knew I had been bitten by a tsetse fly. And anything, I knew, could be a warning sign of cancer.

The only reason I survived medical school was the fact that we always had a new disease to memorize. We never stayed on any one subject long enough for me to really fixate on it. Once I had taken one exam I quickly forgot that set of symptoms and moved on to the next.

I thought about this the last time I was sick. I was lying in my bed, listening to the beating of a bass drum in my temples and feeling the incredible weight of the blanket against my chest. I could feel millions of infectious particles invading my system. Every time I tried to lift my arms I found someone had tied them to the bed with elastic bungee cords, snapping them back down. I couldn't even read because someone had filled all of the empty spaces on the page with small, hollow dots that danced around the words. And when I looked in the mirror I saw a scene from *Terminator 2,* where Arnold Schwartzenegger was losing large chunks of his face before melting into a pool of molten slag.

Part of me knew what was happening: I had the flu. In a few days I would get over it, just like I tell my patients every day.

But part of me knew different. That constant drip, drip from my nose was obviously the slow leaking of cerebrospinal fluid from the opening near my brain, forced out by rising pressure caused by meningitis. My arms and legs were aching because my muscles were being turned into liquid, releasing proteins that would soon clog up my kidneys. My coughing was a sign of pneumonia, making me fight for every gasp of air. Sure, I had the flu, but that wasn't the only reason someone could have chest pains. What a cruel irony that I would catch a virus at the exact same time that I was having a heart attack.

The smart thing would have been to just lie there in my misery and wait quietly for death, but instead, I did what most doctors do when they are sick. I tried to go to work.

This was a bad idea, and shows that I was having trouble thinking clearly. I always feel some sense of duty to go into the office, even if I am sick, but it is not fair to anyone. Most patients have their own germs; they don't need to pick up any more from the doctor.

Actually, there was only one good reason to go to work that day: that's where all the medicine is. If I keeled over on the floor at home, my chances would be a lot worse. The only kind of specialized care I would receive would be when my dog started licking my face. At work there are a lot of other doctors around who could step in and save my life if necessary. What better place to be sick?

It didn't work, of course. The nurses picked up on subtle clues that I was ill, like dropping my stethoscope in my coffee cup or trying to examine a standing lamp. They soon sent me home to recover, and I spent the next few days in bed, listening to the bass drum and being crushed by the blankets. And, just like I always promise my patients, I got better on my own. After a few days my cough cleared up, my muscles felt better, and the bass drum finally stopped pounding. All that was left was a slight headache.

"Uh-oh," I said to myself as I thumbed through my neurology textbooks, "I hope I don't have mad cow disease."

Holiday Time

Every December I find myself running out of time for all my Christmas preparations, including sending cards, buying gifts, and untangling my Christmas lights from last year.

My wife loves Christmas lights. I like them, too, but I wouldn't put them up for myself. I would just look at everyone else's. The only time I ever see our own lights is during that brief moment while pulling into the garage.

But she likes them, so I put them up. This is not an easy job, mostly because when I took them down, sometime in March, I threw each individual fifty-foot strand into the same large box. Evidently, it never occurred to me that Christmas would come back again.

Now over the months, the strands have twisted and mutated, becoming a snarled knot of wires and pointy little bulbs. I can't even find the little plugs on the ends—they have disappeared somewhere into a Bermuda Triangle of Christmas lights. It will take eleven of the twelve days of Christmas just to untangle them. Last year I finally pulled them apart and got them turned on just as people started arriving for Christmas Eve dinner.

Are You a Real Doctor?

It's not my fault. Time just goes too fast before Christmas. Pre-Christmas hours go by faster than any other unit of time, including vacations and time spent in dentist offices waiting for oral surgery. Recent research studies using the calendar on our refrigerator show that December is getting shorter every year. It is now down to about one week, shorter than that if you have to mail any packages.

When I was a kid it took a full twelve months for Christmas to come—if you started counting on Thanksgiving. The season began when the Sears toy catalog arrived, and we were convinced we would get old and die before Santa finally made it. My brother and sisters used to make long chains of safety pins to mark time. We would remove one with each passing day, using it to poke each other when we realized how far we still had to go.

Now, as a grown-up, Thanksgiving and Christmas occur simultaneously. There is no time for anything, like shopping. Every year I make a stack of Christmas catalogs with the page corners turned down, each one marking a page with the exact perfect gift for someone, only it quickly becomes too late to call. Then I have to try to find the same exact item in stores, where they will have one left in size 52 with a button missing. And that doesn't even count the time I spend trying to find a gift for my mother.

Plus, I have to buy "insurance" gifts. These are for people I never see, the ones who leave Happy Holidays cards attached to my newspapers and garbage cans. These cards probably do not represent any kind of veiled threat. Still, it's like the fire department calling and asking for a donation—I'm sure it would never in a million, billion years affect the service you receive, but you won't sleep well if you ignore them.

Without time to shop, I generally have to grab something at the last minute, when only drug stores are open. Last year, for example, I gave nasal dilator strips, those little tapes people wear on their noses during marathons and aerobics classes. This is the perfect gift for someone you have never met. It shows you care—what could be more personal than nasal passages?—but not too much. And unlike prescription medicine, another great last-minute gift idea, there are no pesky side effects, unless they stick them inside their nose by mistake.

If I ever do see these people, I will know instantly if they are using my gift. It's like taking the hideous wedding present out of the closet when your Aunt comes to visit—they would have to stick them on their noses whenever they come to the house. This will give me a chuckle every morning as I climb up to the rain gutter to get my newspaper.

While I'm up there, I'll be able to hang my Christmas lights. To save time, I won't even bother untangling them. I'll just hang them up that way, in one large, glowing ball that spins gently as it hangs from the garage roof and sends a warm, heartfelt message of holiday cheer to all who pass by: Merry Disco Christmas, everyone!

Crazy for Cholesterol

I was really hoping to make it through this book without another column on cholesterol, but I can see I was only fooling myself.

It's not my fault, honest. I don't like thinking about this stuff any more than you do, but they keep changing the rules. Remember oat bran? Remember olive oil? After teasing us with promising research, new studies now show that these things are no better for your cholesterol than any other kind of greasy fiber.

Now, with most of the book under our belts, it's time to bring it (cholesterol) up again, and take another look at the whole confusing problem.

Cholesterol is bad. Everyone should have a blood test to make sure their total cholesterol level is below 200.

No, wait, it's not the total cholesterol. It's the LDL part, the bad cholesterol, that's the problem. Everyone should have a low LDL, or else they're in big trouble.

Did I say LDL? Sorry, I meant HDL. That's the important thing. The HDL is "good cholesterol," one of those oxymorons like "jumbo shrimp." Good cholesterol helps prevent heart attacks, so the higher the HDL, the better.

HAH! Psych! It's not the HDL at all, but the ratio of cholesterol total to HDL cholesterol that really means anything. Forget the rest of that stuff. Everyone should memorize this number for comparisons at dinner parties and holiday gatherings.

Those with bad numbers needs to watch their diet and carefully limit their total dietary intake of cholesterol. I mean fat. Fat turns into cholesterol inside the body. The less you eat, the lower the cholesterol, although it generally takes more than just switching to "Reduced Fat" Chocolate Fudge Supreme Brownie Cookies. If the cholesterol is high enough, the doctor may even prescribe an expensive cholesterol medicine to bring it down, which will protect the patient from scary things like heart attacks and strokes.

Unless it doesn't. Last month a new study showed that people over seventy get no benefit from using medicine to control their cholesterol. There was no connection between high cholesterol and heart attacks in this group, and taking the medicine made no difference in life expectancy.

Maybe older people just handle cholesterol better. Maybe making it to seventy weeds out people who had premature heart attacks in their fifties (although I'm sure every heart attack seems premature at the time). Maybe the medicine just doesn't work on anyone who remembers Dwight Eisenhower. At least for this group, high-priced cholesterol medicines may give them nothing but side effects.

You see? No wonder people are confused. Luckily, there is a way to stay out of trouble.

Remember, medicine is not the only way to control cholesterol. It is not even the best way. Cholesterol drugs are just an expensive, semi-hazardous way to correct something that people do to themselves. Think of them as the antidote to Double Whoppers with cheese. We probably wouldn't need them at all if humans had naturally occurring antibodies to dangerous things like fettuccine Alfredo. One cholesterol expert has even suggested putting measured doses of cholesterol-lowering drugs directly into hamburger meat, allowing people to break even. (No one is really doing this. In fact, this may be one of the few prescription medicines not found in hamburger.)

While there are some rare genetic syndromes that can cause high cholesterol, 90 percent of these people would be helped, if not fixed, by eating less fat. Or just eating less, period. This is proved again every time someone with high cholesterol is stranded at sea without red meat or Snickers bars, and they come back fifty pounds lighter with a cholesterol level the same as their shoe size.

Without this kind of diet control, a lot of people will just have to rely on medicine to lower their cholesterol and their risk for heart disease. They won't be alone. Mevacor, the most popular cholesterol medicine, is now third on the list of most prescribed drugs in the country, and costs about $2 a pill. Some people have to take two a day, at least until doctors change their minds again and decide that the most important thing is actually the level of VLDL (Very LDL, the really, really bad cholesterol) divided by the blood sugar and multiplied by the first three digits of your phone number, as adjusted for ambient humidity.

Some things never change.

Sit-Down Doctor

It's hard to find a doctor.

Not just finding one—that's easy. Turn around at a hospital or golf course, and there we are. No, I mean finding one to take care of your medical problems.

This is harder than it sounds. In the old days you could just ask your friends for advice, although there were no guarantees. Your friend might think his doctor is Marcus Welby, whereas you see only Freddy Krueger in a white coat.

Plus, while doctors are sworn to confidentiality, there was always the chance of running into someone you know in the waiting room, requiring a fast, safe lie ("Well, I've been having trouble with my . . . um . . . my ear").

These days, most people don't choose their own doctors. Their insurance companies do. They receive a list of approved names, and they have to select one to take care of their family.

You can't tell a lot from a name. To find out more you have to actually get sick and go, and by then it's too late. You could waste

Are You a Real Doctor?

two or three illnesses on a doctor you don't even like.

I have a friend who likes to interview doctors ahead of time, to see if they will be compatible. This is a good idea, but it could easily fill up a doctor's entire day with chatting and having tea. Believe me, most doctors are not out playing golf. They are trying to take care of the patients they already have and still make it home in time to tuck in their kids.

Instead, some clinics are now putting photos of their doctors in the lobby. This lets you recognize them when they come into the room, so you know it's not the maintenance guy. Unfortunately, once you are wearing a gown that opens in the back you are largely committed to the appointment, no matter what the doctor looks like.

Appearance is not the best way to select a doctor. I know one doctor who wore a Star Trek uniform for his lobby photo. As you might imagine, this attracts a certain type of life-form as a patient. Luckily, most of these people do not mind having a doctor who would be kicked off the Whitewater jury on the first day.

Now the latest thing is the computerized doctor database. This provides detailed information about the doctors on the list, giving their academic background and special interests. Like any computer, it depends entirely on input, which means it gives a complete and accurate description of any doctors who bothered to fill out the form.

There is also the Doctor Referral Line, where you can call and specify the kind of doctor you want, and they will give you a name and help you set up an appointment.

I wondered how this works, so one day I disguised my voice (like they would know) and called them, trying to get referred to myself. I couldn't get me. They kept sending me to one of my partners. I asked for a doctor "in the Brooklyn Center area," and then, "a family doctor who does some sports medicine," and then, "someone with a beard and a name that rhymes with 'bark.' " No luck.

Finally I just asked for me directly. They said I wasn't taking any patients. I would have gone home, except that my office was full of people who hadn't bothered to check with the referral line.

Sit-Down Doctor

Now compare these flashy, high-tech methods with this ad my mom found in a small Florida newspaper: "OLD-FASHIONED DOCTOR. Sits down and listens to you. Wants a few more good patients."

The ad was placed by Dr. R. Sliker, who has been in practice for thirty years. He was surprised that another doctor would be interested in his ad, especially one in Minnesota. "I'm no rocket scientist when it comes to advertising," he told me on the phone. "It's just my style. People will tell you what's wrong with them if you just listen."

Still, when patient surveys list the things people look for in their doctors, "sitting down" always comes out on top. According to patients, doctors are always in a rush. They make brief cameo appearances before zooming off to answer calls or order more tests. When they take time to sit down, it makes patients feel worthwhile.

How much do you need to know? Patients don't generally care what doctors look like, or where they went to school. With medicine being run by huge corporations, they just want someone who will sit down and listen to them.

Luckily, this doesn't mean going to Florida. There are doctors sitting down all over the country. Check the list, ask their other patients, or drop by the office and feel for warm spots on the chairs. If they sit down, then they may be all right.

Either that, or they're just tired from all that golf.

Back to School

There I was, sitting with a bunch of students in my college cafeteria, drinking coffee and complaining about merciless teachers, impossible assignments, and unforgiving deadlines, all in an effort to avoid doing any actual work.

While this could have been a couple of decades ago, it was actually a lot more recent. I was back at Augsburg College, my alma mater, to find out what college students today are thinking.

I need to know because I had been chosen to give the commencement speech at Augsburg, a tremendous honor for a columnist who mostly writes about killer mutant lice and low-fat Twinkies. I was thrilled when they asked me to speak, even though I have to wear a black muumuu and a hat that looks like a record album cover (the Beatles' legendary *Black Album*).

Of course, students today are from the CD generation, and some of them have never seen a record album. This was my problem. It's been almost twenty years since I graduated from college. While not yet a codger, I have become at least an old guy.

What do I know about college life? I don't know which one is Hootie and which one is Butthead. I can't understand why anyone would tear holes in their jeans on purpose. I have to turn off the sound during the musical guests on Letterman, the bands with names like Hemorrhaging Marsupials. It causes me physical pain to write this, as if my brain were undergoing twenty years of fossilization all at once, but to me, their music just sounds like a bunch of noise.

Here is the proof: I have no idea why kids wear their baseball caps backwards, and, like any old guy, I want them to stop it.

Still, I wanted to give a good speech, one that would mean something to graduating students. I wanted it to be more relevant than a Special Graduation Weekend Sale at Palmquist Patio Furniture and Pool Supply.

Being out of touch, there was only one way to find out what students were thinking: ask them. Before the speech I spent a few days walking around campus with a tape recorder, asking students what they thought I should talk about.

Many of them were feeling anxious about the next phase in their lives, whatever it might be. In high school, you worry about college. In college, you worry about grad school or getting a job. In grad school you worry about losing government funding for bizarre research projects like heterozygous whisker transplants in genetically engineered mice. Anyone who goes to medical school can understand these feelings, especially since most of us never even get real jobs until we are almost thirty.

Some students were having problems with their classes, especially organic chemistry. I could understand this, too. I spent a year of my life whining about organic chemistry. I blamed bad teachers and textbooks for my own inability to accept the idea that we are all just bunches of carbon atoms in particularly lively arrangements.

Some students were mad about college rules and red tape, especially the rules that prevent you from graduating until you pay all your fees, even the ones left over from simple freshman-year mishaps that destroy entire racks of glass beakers in the chemistry lab, causing insignificant, easily controlled fires with only minimal property damage. Instantly, I could relate.

A lot of them were taking classes they hated but were necessary for graduation. They were convinced they would never need to know anything about these required subjects unless, as I pointed out, they were lucky enough to get their own newspaper columns so they could make fun of them.

And one person told me this when I asked him what to say at graduation: "You're the speaker. You figure it out. That's your job." This is exactly what I would have said to some old guy bothering me in the college cafeteria.

Clearly, as much as college has changed, a lot of it is still the same. College students complain about the same stuff we used to complain about. They worry about the same things that scared us.

Evidently, I am more in tune than I thought. College life was coming back to me. In fact, after a few short hours on campus I experienced a weird, time-warp effect where I suddenly got nervous and thought, "Oh, no, what time is it? I gotta get to class!"

I had become one with the graduating class. I could relate to them easily, graduate to undergraduate, old guy to young person. This eased my mind, allowing me to craft an insightful, moving, and highly original graduation speech ("The future lies ahead . . .").

And, while I didn't tear any holes in the knees of my gown (it was a rental), I hope people in the audience took a close look at my hat. In a gesture of unity and solidarity with my matriculating brothers and sisters, I wore my record album backwards.

Quick! To the Bloodmobile!

No matter how much you like your job, there are days when going to work can leave you feeling drained. This was especially true the day the bloodmobile came to our office.

To be honest, I wasn't planning on giving blood. It's hard to find time during the day, and for some reason the blood bank does not accept night deposits. The bloodmobile, basically a large converted Winnebago, solves this problem by bringing the blood bank to you, making blood donation easy.

In fact, the hardest part may be the written exam. Before you can donate an aide asks you about your medical history, including a list of about a hundred different rare diseases. While many of the names were familiar, I had forgotten all about diseases like babesiosis, which I assume affects your voice and makes you sound like a talking pig.

They also ask how you slept the night before, and whether you ate any breakfast. Now you know: giving blood is like visiting your mother. They also want to know if you have any tattoos, probably to find out how you handle pain. Giving blood should be a snap after getting "ZZ Top" inscribed on your bottom.

If you correctly answer all the questions, you move on to the nurses, who test your blood anyway. They check your blood type, poking a finger and mixing a drop of blood with several pool chemicals on a glass slide. Then comes the hemoglobin test, where they put a drop in a tube and watch it rise and fall like a miniature lava lamp. Later they will do more tests to make sure the blood is safe, like HIV, hepatitis, viscosity, octane rating, and robust bouquet ("Vital, yet never presumptuous") tests.

They then lead you to a dentist's chair with one arm rest. The nurses are friendly and cheerful—very cheerful, in fact, for people who will soon be poking you with sharp objects.

They give you juice, which you can drink during the donation process. I picked cranberry juice, thinking no one would notice if some of it ran right through me into the bag.

The nurse paints your inner arm orange, the most hygienic color, and then, finally, comes the needle.

There is a great debate about whether you should look at the needle or turn away. I prefer to watch. This allows me to use my cool, objective medical demeanor, while pretending it is happening to someone I don't like. This particular time I chose Newt Gingrich, although the illusion was shattered when actual human blood came out.

You can then relax and talk to the other bleeders, unless of course you faint. They get one or two fainters a day, except at high schools. There a kind of mass hysteria takes over. The students see one person faint, and pretty soon they are dropping like acorns, even during the written test.

Of course, the nurses are ready. At the first sign of greenish tint they envelop you in a blanket of cheerfulness. "Oh, it's just fine, we're not fainting at all, we're doing so well, everything is going fine . . ." Meanwhile they are putting your feet up, your head back, and hitting you with enough smelling salts to arouse a sponge. They told me they would never just take the blood while someone was unconscious, even though it would make the whole process a lot easier.

Quick! To the Bloodmobile!

The blood, about two cups, runs though a long tube into a pre-labeled baggie. The clear plastic bag feels warm when it is full, as if you have given them the very essence of life. Then they clamp it and toss it in a freezer.

You are rewarded with a fluorescent green or hot pink wrap-around bandage, plugging the leak and making doubly sure that everyone knows you gave. In three days your blood could be inside a person who needs it. Separated into the various component cells, it could save two or three lives by the time your arm heals.

As if this weren't reward enough, you also get cookies. Not cheap ones, either, but name brands like Oreos and Lorna Doones. I don't normally eat Oreos, because I suspect the white stuff in the middle is the exact same substance found in coronary arteries during bypass surgery, but I did that day. I figure if you only eat them after giving blood, you'll be fine. You'd be anemic long before you got fat.

Thanks to the bloodmobile, giving blood was fast, easy, and even a little exciting. And besides everything else, I got to lie down for twenty minutes during work. If that doesn't make it all worthwhile, I don't know what would.

Health to the Chief

Like many teenagers getting ready for summer camp, President Clinton had his annual checkup in the spring.

According to the White House, the president went through three hours of tests during his physical. I can't even think of that many tests to do on someone. A normal checkup would never take that long, unless you were trying to document someone actually gaining weight.

The results were reported in newspapers and on TV everywhere. So much for patient confidentiality. White House sources claim that Clinton, who turned fifty this year, is in better shape now than he was last year. His weight is unchanged at 216 pounds—big, but not Pavarotti. People would probably never even notice except he likes to wear those skimpy little running shorts that look like they belong to Robert Reich instead.

Press Secretary Mike McCurry also bragged about the president's cholesterol level, which has dropped from 203 to 191. This was reported as a startling, major news story, particularly since

Health to the Chief

photos from the previous day showed the president enjoying a massive lunch of steak, chicken, ribs, *and* meatloaf.

Normally, to get this kind of drop in cholesterol you would have to exercise and eat right, or just have the test done twice. Cholesterol tests can vary by ten or twenty points each time you do them. A drop of twelve points means about as much as switching to Sara Lee "Lite" Cheesecake so you can have a second helping.

Still, according to the White House, these tests conclusively prove that President Clinton is in perfect physical condition to run the country, fix the deficit, adopt a child, and, coincidentally, run for reelection. The subtle, underlying message is: Bill Clinton is young, and, nyahh nyahh, Bob Dole is not.

They didn't need a doctor to tell us that. High cholesterol is one risk factor for heart disease, but the biggest risk factor of all is age. Bob Dole has already surpassed the life expectancy for white males in this country, not to mention the mandatory retirement age for federal employees. This means that even if he gets the job, we may have to let him go.

Faced with this risk factor gap, Dole could only wave his cholesterol results, along with a photo of himself on a treadmill wearing his own skimpy shorts, in an effort to look presidential. This was a truly frightening image, making all of America wonder the same thing: "What ever happened to Miss Hathaway from the Beverly Hillbillies, and why have we never seen them together?"

Most people don't need annual checkups anymore. Myself, I would never want to do a physical on the president. If running shorts are not flattering, imagine how he would look in a gown that opens in the back.

I can't imagine checking the presidential ears, tonsils, or listening to the presidential heart beat. Not to mention the more revealing, personal aspects of a physical. ("All right, Mr. President, please change your mind and cough.")

Some parts of an examination, while accepted medical procedures, could appear menacing to the untrained eye. Any alert secret service agent would have no choice but to throw himself in front of the rubber glove while others wrestled the doctor to the ground.

Are You a Real Doctor?

Actually, the most important part of any checkup is the nagging. This is where the doctor tells you to stop smoking, eat right, exercise every day, and so forth. This doesn't make interesting headlines, but it can do a lot more for someone's health than ordering a million blood tests and X-rays.

This would be the really tough part. How could you nag the president? You would be ordering the leader of the free world to wear his seat belt, get more sleep, and, if he is going to be sexually active, be sure to practice safe sex.

I hope this president already knows some of these things. After all, he already knows how important it is to exercise. He just needs some baggier shorts and, the next time he feels like lunch, to maybe do without the meatloaf.

All Alone on Career Day

When the counselors from the junior high school called and asked me to come to career day, I thought it would be fun. It would be a chance to talk to some teenagers about being a doctor. Surely, a lot of them must be thinking about careers in medicine, I told myself. They must have a lot of questions. I said I would be happy to come.

I showed up early, hoping to get a good spot in the gym. I was led to a cafeteria table with a paper sign taped on the front. "PHYSICIAN," it said in bold letters printed in magic marker.

A few minutes later, the kids arrived. As it turned out, they did have a lot of questions. Here is the question they asked me most often: "How long do you have to go to school to become . . . a vet?"

Of course, not everyone wanted to be a veterinarian. Some of them asked about dental school. One wanted to know the difference between a psychologist and a psychiatrist. Several wanted to be physical therapists, or occupational therapists, or whichever one gets to meet professional football players in the locker room. One confused student even asked me about being a professional wrestler. I told him that Dr. Destroyer was not an official professional title.

The one thing they never asked me about was becoming a doctor. I decided to steer the conversation a bit, in case they were just shy. The results were even less promising.

"You go to school for *how long*?" Two young girls in black New Kids on the Block T-shirts were listening to me talk about the years of college, medical school, and the residency, and they could not hide their amazement.

"That's unreal!" one of them said out loud. "I could never do that. By the time I got done, I'd be *old*."

I thought about it as they walked over to the computer programming display. OK, looking back it seems like a long time. But it went fast. Even if I hadn't gone to medical school, I would still be exactly this old now. Of course, I started college before either of them was born, and I was in school for more years than they have been alive. I know they would never believe that old age will happen to them, too.

Another student had trouble with the nature of the work. "You cut people up?" he asked. "Gross! I could never be a doctor."

I tried to explain that different kinds of doctors do different things. It had been years since I cut up a whole person, but some days I might remove a little piece of one, if there was a good reason. This same teenager could probably sit through a triple feature of *Friday the 13th* movies and never even blink, but he walked away from my table holding his stomach.

A few of the kids eyed me suspiciously. "Are you a real doctor?" one of them asked. I have heard that same question hundreds of times, often from my own family. My sisters can't quite believe it, either.

It was becoming clear that no one attending Career Day wanted to ask about my career. I took a look around the room, watching to see where the kids were spending their time.

My assigned spot was between the fire fighter and the jet pilot. Groups of young people were gathered around both of those tables. Through spaces in the crowd I could catch a glimpse of axes and gas

All Alone on Career Day

masks, alongside a real fighter plane helmet resting on the table in front of the pilot.

Maybe that was the problem. I had no props. I was there alone, without my medical bag or even a stethoscope. I should have brought something to show them. Granted, there wasn't much I could do to compete with such a cool helmet. No one wants to see a bunch of syringes and a bottle of measles vaccine.

I realized it would be hard to explain why I like being a doctor so much. To really show someone I would have to take them with me for an entire day. I would have to take them to the nursery to see a newborn, or to the intensive care unit to comfort a dying patient, or to the high school across the street to do sports physicals for a few hours. If they could see, even in a single day, how doctors can become a part of their patients' lives, then they would understand.

Across the country, enrollment to medical school has been falling off. There are now fewer than two applicants for every spot, an all-time low level of interest. I figured I better try harder.

Just then a young man approached my table. He seemed anxious to talk to me. I smiled, knowing at least one person in the room had a question for me. Now was my chance to do whatever I could to make that person see what a great job I had.

"Do you have a brown car?" he asked. "I think maybe you left your lights on."

Death Mail

People turning forty are often overwhelmed by thoughts of their own mortality, questioning their place in the great scheme of life. And that's before they receive the brochure from the funeral parlor.

When I turned forty, it was not an easy time. Doctors are just like anyone—maybe worse, since they know all the various things that can go wrong. Every doctor has seen patients who hit forty and, like cars that go two odometer clicks past the 50,000-mile warranty, suddenly fall apart.

Still, I was doing pretty well until I checked the mail. There I found a sales brochure from a local mortuary. "Give your loved ones the gift of love," it said. This turned out to be not a diamond but a preplanned, pre-paid funeral, your own, before you go. (My advice: Charge it.)

This was easily the most frightening piece of mail I had ever received that did not have Ed McMahon's picture on it. It is certainly not the kind of thing you want to receive as you approach a milestone birthday.

The brochure came with a return mail card that said, "Detach and mail today!" The worst part was the exclamation point. Evidently, I had little time to lose: Act now! Or else!

To demonstrate sensitivity, there was also a disclaimer on the front that read, "It is our sincere apology if this should reach a home where a death has recently occurred." Why apologize? This has to be their ideal target market. Who would benefit more from some helpful information about funeral planning?

Anyone turning forty is much more likely to just get upset. Believe me, I didn't need their friendly reminder that I was now one step closer to death.

For years I have been keeping a list of my own body parts that are wearing out. With replacement parts so hard to come by, all you can really do is learn to adjust your lifestyle to make up for them. For example, years ago I learned how to gently pull on the corners of my eyes and squint when I need to read traffic signs at night. (This would be a much better trick if it left one hand free to hold the steering wheel.)

I have lots of little tricks like that. Your individual results may vary, but they work for me. I never lie with my feet pointing downward, or I would wake up with terrible cramps in them. I brush my teeth right after eating ice cream so I don't get a toothache. I never kneel on a hard floor because my knees would sound like two pans of Jiffy Pop for the rest of the day.

It's like living in the same house for many years. After a while you naturally accommodate for certain things. You learn to jiggle the key a certain way, or how to give the basement door a shove, or to let the bathroom faucet run for a while before drinking.

Actually, I have been very lucky. I can still do most of the active sports I enjoy. The difference is in the recovery period. It takes me about three days to recover from strenuous activities like sweeping or putting a box on the high shelf in the garage. Going by my experience, any forty-year-old who runs a marathon or goes bungee jumping will spend the next year and a half just getting over it.

Still, forty is officially "middle age," not "almost dead." Why send me a recruiting pamphlet? Did the mortuary people know something?

I called them to find out. They claimed they didn't even know my birthday was coming. According to a parlor spokesperson, the leaflet was just part of a mass mailing. They were blanketing the area with burial circulars to build "name awareness" for their services.

The funeral business, an $8 billion industry, has been changing. While the individual death rate in the country is the same—still 100 percent and holding—people are no longer choosing the traditional, more expensive services. Some funeral homes now offer—honest—drive-through visitations. Many customers choose cremation or rented caskets, which can kill profits.

Evidently, morticians are no longer willing to wait until we come to them. They are coming after us, at least by mail.

I think they should keep the newly forty off the mailing list. Many of us are already pretty touchy. A burial pamphlet could push us over the edge.

Besides, there are plenty of much older people around. Take Ed McMahon. Judging by his picture, the man is at least 100, which may mean it's time for him to get some junk mail of his own for a change.

Rating the Nielsens

I've been under a lot of stress recently, making hundreds of critical, split-second decisions that could mean the difference between life and death—for TV shows. It's our job. For one week, at least, we were . . . a Nielsen family.

We started getting postcards from Nielsen Television Research a few weeks ago, letting us know we had been selected as a Nielsen TV Household. This meant we had a chance to give feedback to "the people who plan TV programs." This is surprising to anyone who thought most TV programs came to life by random chance, like lightning striking primordial ooze.

Naturally, I had heard of the Nielsen ratings. I always assumed the Nielsen people came out to your home and attached some high-tech black box to your TV that monitored your viewing habits. This would send a signal to Nielsen Central Command whenever you switched from Dave to Jay, usually when the musical guest, always the loudest new-wave grunge band they could find, began to play.

Instead, what we got was a diary. It is a little booklet full of detailed charts and spaces that break down an entire week into fifteen-minute increments. Filling out the diary is much more work than actually watching TV, even with cable.

There are columns to record the name of the programs, the channel number and station name, and whether the TV was on or off during this period. (Research shows that watching with the set off is much less harmful.) There is even a place to mark if your TV was on but no one was watching, although in that case I think you only get partial credit.

In this way you are supposed to write down every TV show watched by anyone in your house for a full week. There was a crisp one-dollar bill in the packet, as "a token of appreciation" for doing this.

This explains a lot. The only people providing feedback are the ones who think doing this much work for a dollar is a good deal, like five-year-olds. No wonder some programs are popular, like those home video shows that are basically sixty minutes of people falling down. The top-rated show in the country could soon be *Wishbone*, which features a dog dressing up as various figures from classic literature.

Evidently, the entire content of television, which sadly has more influence on some people than government, school, or family, is determined by a handful of people across the country who have way too much spare time on their hands.

Obviously, being a Nielsen household is an incredible responsibility, much too important for us to record the shows we really watch. I don't want the TV people to know that we watch *Xena: Warrior Princess* every time it comes on, which, thanks to cable, is seventeen times a week.

We don't always go looking for it; sometimes we come across it while browsing. We use TV as the video equivalent of a police band scanner. And the fact that we watch a show is no guarantee of quality. Sometimes we find awful, horrible programs, which we watch in their entirety to make fun of them.

There is no place in the diary to record this, just like there is no place to list the shows you actively avoid watching. This is like voting against the candidate you hate. For a long time I watched whatever was on opposite *Roseanne,* just hoping someone would finally get the message.

Actually, except for *Xena,* we really didn't watch much TV that week. Most of the time our VCR watches TV for us. It's a tremendous time saver. We set it to record the shows we like, then we stack the tapes on a shelf and never watch them. Eventually we forget which tapes have TV shows and which have our wedding video or exclusive footage of our infant son taking a bath in the sink. Then we go buy more tapes.

I couldn't let the Nielsen people know this. Instead, I kept a list of the shows we would have watched if we weren't so busy, shows like *Masterpiece Theater* and *The McNeil/Lehrer News Hour,* although I think they changed the name when one of the main guys, I forget which one, quit.

Whichever, he's retired now, with plenty of time on his hands, which means he should be the one keeping a Nielsen diary, not me. I'll stick with medicine. The truth is, I can't handle the pressure.

Everyday Olympics

The torch is no longer burning, but Olympic fever, like a big-budget Coca-Cola commercial, is still around.

For two weeks every election year, the entire country watches the Olympics, tuning in each evening to experience the incredible drama and suspense of sporting events held earlier that day. When the acting surgeon general, whoever it is, told Americans to get in at least thirty minutes of vigorous activity each day, I'm pretty sure she didn't mean on NBC.

In all fairness, not all of these people knew what was happening. Many of them believed they were watching "must see TV," barely noticing that Seinfeld and the gang were running around in shorts and track shoes, probably in one of Kramer's wacky schemes.

The daily coverage focused on the most important news from the games: the number of gold medals won by Americans. This allowed us to wave huge foam fingers and chant "we're number one," as if we had all spent the last four years training to get ready. Winning a gold medal takes years of dedication, commitment, and sacrifice, all so that the rest of us can take credit while sitting in front of the TV with a bowl of Pringles and a Diet Pepsi.

Watching other people exercise is the real American pastime. We all want to know who is the fastest person in the world, even if we don't know who is the fastest person in the neighborhood.

Or even in the house. I'm pretty sure I could beat my wife, although in fifteen years the only time we ever raced was down the aisle. I won because I wanted to reach the minister before she came to her senses. I can beat my son in a sprint, although being five and in perpetual motion he would definitely have the edge in any sort of distance event.

It wasn't always like this. In junior high, everyone knew who was fastest. In our class it was Nancy "Mouse" Iverson, a girl who was cute, nice, and could run like a gazelle being chased by cheetahs. Her speed was eventually taken for granted; it became her special niche in the junior high scheme of life. You could have asked any random kid in the hall, and they knew Nancy was the one to beat.

As a kid, you always know which of your friends is the fastest, or the strongest, or can jump high or throw far. You learn because you have to, if only to avoid messing with the wrong person. Once you know who is fast, you never try to race them to the bus. Instead, you just punch them in the arm from behind.

Now, as a grown-up, I have no idea who is faster than I am. I look around my office and wonder: Could I beat Deb, my nurse, in a race? Would the individual receptionists trounce me in Graco-Roman wrestling? Can I jump higher than the other doctors? Who can throw the farthest? Who is the fastest? These questions rarely come up in an average day, unless you need something from a high shelf, but I feel it is important to know.

We need some of that Olympic spirit in everyday life. Not another full-fledged Olympics—we certainly don't need more John Tesh—but some simple games that would let us test each other and learn some answers.

Of course, for people to participate such games would have to take place at work. Everyone says they are too busy to exercise

Are You a Real Doctor?

(except the president of the United States), but nobody is ever too busy to go to work. Olympic-style contests could be a part of job performance reviews, like those physical fitness tests we had to do every year in gym class. ("Bill, I'm thinking of promoting you. Last one to the water cooler is a junior partner.")

I'm not talking about javelins flying around the office, or high hurdles in front of the coffee pot. To encourage everyone to play we could make up some common, everyday events, like the crumpled paper wastebasket toss. Or stapler opening, which takes the same strength and stamina as the decathlon. We get so much junk mail at work that emptying my box is like doing the clean-and-jerk power lift.

People are already trained for events like these. They just need those skimpy uniforms that ride up in the back. If they can make Olympic events out of orb dancing or Busby Berkeley-style swimming in circles, why not more practical events? Everyone knows that the Olympics were first started by ancient Greeks who would run twenty-six miles to return a video before closing.

In the Everyday Olympics, everyone participates. That way, we can take credit for any gold medals with a clean conscience.

Call your international Olympic committee or human resources department to set up some games right away, before the fever dies down. If you have to, offer to wrestle them for it.

My Doctor, the Son

I grew up in Brooklyn Center, a suburb of Minneapolis. My parents moved there when I was two. They still live there, at least during the warmer months in Minnesota.

By a strange twist of fate, I now practice medicine in Brooklyn Center. I did not plan to return—I applied at this clinic, they had an opening at this office, and I took it. Now that I am back, though, it does mean that my practice is a little different from most.

My office is about two miles from our old house. From the parking lot I can see the shopping center where I had my first job at age sixteen, busing tables at a restaurant that has long since closed. Another story in this book tells about being the team physician for my old high school. Some of my patients are people who knew me a long time ago, before I ever wore a white coat or even a tie.

And my mom and dad stop by once in a while.

My parents are now patients at our clinic, which means that they come to the office for routine visits and lab tests. They also come at other times, like when they are shopping at the mall or just passing by.

The nurses and receptionists are pretty used to seeing them. They just wave as my parents pass through the lobby on their way back to my office or exam rooms. Once in a while a new employee will give them a worried look, but they soon learn to recognize the smiling woman with the gray hair and the man with the accent.

Because of this, I usually have no warning that they are coming until I step out of an exam room and see them standing there. Sometimes I almost get whiplash from switching roles so fast.

"You remember what I said, Mrs. Wilson," I will be telling a patient in my most authoritative doctor voice. "You're going to have to take better care of yourself."

The patient will nod seriously as she watches me leave the room. She gathers her things and steps out into the hallway, only to see me happily greeting an older couple. "Hi, Mom. Hi, Dad," I say, giving them a hug. At that point I'm sure my voice, which was so stern a moment ago, has lost some of its authority.

What do patients think when they see my parents in the office? I'm sure they realize I must have a mother. They may not have expected to meet her during their annual checkup, but it's not like it's a secret.

Fortunately, I have never been a doctor who relies on rigid appearances. While I try to be professional, "formal" is not a word that describes my practice style. Most of the time I take a personal interest in my patients and their families. It is probably fair that they get to experience mine.

Besides, I already share a practice with my wife, and our son spends some time at our office on occasion. Having my parents there seems only natural. This is family practice, after all. We just take the concept a little farther than most people do.

So my folks stop by when they can. So far, no matter how hectic things are, or how busy I am, I have always been glad to see them.

Sometimes we go to lunch. More often they bring food with them, especially when my wife and I are both working late. They pick up our son during the occasional daycare crisis, and watch our dog when we go out of town. For many years they helped me survive college, and medical school, and residency. Now that I am out on my own, a doctor, they are still helping me.

I try to do what I can for them. I check on their lab results, and help them deal with the pharmacy and insurance companies. As hard as it is, I give them my opinion when medical questions come up. I can't be their doctor—I am much too close to them to be objective. I can only help, acting as an interpreter and guide through a confusing process. At those times, I can only be a son, not a doctor. And that's fine with them—there are a lot of other doctors.

A few years ago my mom tripped and fractured her ankle. Her doctor recommended a cast, and, because I do most of the orthopedic work in our office, I made her one.

She took it on a trip to Europe, walking on it the entire time. "It held up pretty well," she told me when she came back to the office to have it removed. "Next time you should make it a little higher. And tell people to wear a clog on the opposite foot. That way they can walk level."

In a house a few miles away, this same woman first taught me to tie my own shoes. Forty years later, I'm still learning.

NORMANDALE COMMUNITY COLLEGE
LIBRARY
9700 FRANCE AVENUE SOUTH
BLOOMINGTON, MN 55431-4399